START UP
STAND UP

START UP
STAND UP

A STEP-BY-STEP GUIDE TO GROWING YOUR BUSINESS

from your first paying customer to a vibrant user community

NANDINI VAIDYANATHAN

JAICO PUBLISHING HOUSE

Ahmedabad Bangalore Bhopal Bhubaneswar Chennai
Delhi Hyderabad Kolkata Lucknow Mumbai

Published by Jaico Publishing House
A-2 Jash Chambers, 7-A Sir Phirozshah Mehta Road
Fort, Mumbai - 400 001
jaicopub@jaicobooks.com
www.jaicobooks.com

© Nandini Vaidyanathan

START UP, STAND UP
ISBN 978-81-8495-918-5

First Jaico Impression: 2016

Page design and layout: R. Ajith Kumar, Delhi

Dedicated to

*The ottoman at our home in Goa, which served as
my writing space.*

*The panoramic view of our very own French Riviera from our
apartment in Aldeia de Goa.*

*Anil, my life partner, who owns the ottoman, made the view
possible and reinforced my faith in 'all or nothing' (I did not steal
this phrase from Jockey!).*

HOW CAN I THANK YOU GUYS ENOUGH!

THANK YOU, AS always, my mentees and students. You have all made this book possible and you continue to inspire me to think the way I do. Thank you all who read my first book *Entrepedia* and wrote to me about how it helped you start up and changed your life. I count my blessings with happiness, affection and gratitude.

Thank you, Jaico Publishing House for approaching me to write this book. Thank you, Abhishek for connecting with me and gently coaxing me to write this. Thank you Reena Jayswal, my commissioning editor. You are truly amazing in the way you gave your inputs and made this an eminently readable work. A big thanks to your team too.

Thank you Nita for the gorgeous cover design. Thank you Rachna for the wonderful illustrations. Both *Entrepedia* and this book have been immensely embellished by your artistry.

Thank you, Medini for anchoring me when my thoughts went on a random jaunt. Thank you Anil, you were my *Entrepreneur in Residence*. What more could I have asked for?

Thanks to you Appa, the *word* continues to be my *world*.

THE WHY OF THE WHAT!

" **Good judgment comes from experience and a lot of that comes from bad experience** "

– Will Rogers

START UP, STAND UP! is your guide to growing your business. It draws up the blueprint for your journey from acquiring your first paying customer to building an evangelical user community for your products by creating mindshare in them as a go-to brand. It is your Bible, for things you should and should not do – once you hit the market – to grow your business over the next three years. Read on so you can hit the accelerator! It is meant for Indian entrepreneurs but many of the sutras are applicable to any entrepreneur in any part of the world.

It is a stand-alone, independent property and is not a sequel to my first book, *Entrepedia*. I'm saying this because it is not necessary to read *Entrepedia* to understand and internalize *Start up, Stand up!* But if you have read it, you will stand to benefit.

Between 2006 and 2011, I mentored 500 entrepreneurs as a gesture of goodwill, i.e, free of cost. Most of them came to me with a rather nebulous concept that they had in mind and I mentored them to become market-ready. At that time, no one in India had heard of mentorship in the entrepreneurial space. Nor were they prepared to pay for being mentored. Back then, anyone who had grey hair and spoke with élan and confidence was assumed to be wiser than the rest and called a mentor.

In 2011, I thought the market was ready to recognize a mentor as a very critical stakeholder in the Indian entrepreneurial ecosystem and therefore pay for being mentored. So, I founded CARMa with a lofty ambition of changing the karma of entrepreneurs in India.

CARMa, an acronym for Creating Access to Resources and Markets (www.carmaconnect.in), mentors budding entrepreneurs for a small fee And since then, I have mentored over 1500 entrepreneurs from all walks of life in CARMa.

Unlike the first 500 entrepreneurs, who were mostly just starting up, I have mentored even mature enterprises and family businesses in CARMa. I suspect it is about 40 percent startups, 50 percent mature enterprises and 10 percent family businesses.

Over the years, I have developed a proprietary process of mentoring, which is result-oriented, process-driven, mile-stoned and measureable. And to democratize access, I have made it completely online. It is a time-bound program, and I charge a small, one-time upfront fee for it instead of equity, as I don't believe in taking a stake in my mentee's company.

I have called the chapters in this book, CARMa Sutras. Our mentoring program is called CARMa Sutra and I thought it was also a fitting name to give to the chapters in this book, as there is not a word in here that has not been learnt from my mentoring!

As always, the chapter flow is more the way I visualized it. If you want to mix and match, go ahead, but make sure you do address all of them, even if not in the same order.

I have tried to include most of what is relevant to the process of growing your business. If I have left out any, do let me know and I will make sure I include it in the next edition. I have also used *him* to include *her* throughout the book, as under our Constitution, he includes she.

In my TEDX speech in 2011 (which you can check out on YouTube), I had said that entrepreneurship is like Circe (pronounced *kir-kee*), the Greek goddess of magic, who beguiles us, tempts us and seduces us. Since then, if anything, its hold on us has gotten fiercer and its magic stronger around the world in general, but more so in India.

Start up, Stand up! is the product of my mentoring experience. In the process of mentoring 2000 entrepreneurs over a decade and covering more than 300 domains, I have been able to build and share with you an enviably rich, variegated and pulsating library of goof-ups and good practices, misadventures and exhilarating journeys, misdemeanors and textbook fairness, hubris and humility.

My teaching experience too has contributed in no mean measure to this book. When I wrote *Entrepedia* I used to largely offer a course in entrepreneurship to MBA students. Whilst I had fun engaging with yet-untrammelled young minds, I was also frustrated that these young people were not looking at being entrepreneurs in the first place! Their colleges, their parents and their entire universe were obsessed about placements and willy-nilly, so were they.

In each batch, I have a few students who promise me that '*one day*' they will become entrepreneurs, after tucking in some solid work experience and saving some money. Some of them have but not as many as I'd have liked to see.

So for the last three years, I have made it a point to offer the course only to the following categories:

- ❖ Those who already have an idea and opt for my course so that they can build the business model around their idea
- ❖ Those who are frustrated in their corporate careers and are looking to fortify themselves, by way of the course, to take their plunge as entrepreneurs
- ❖ Those who are already entrepreneurs but have discovered that their cash register is not ringing as loudly and as often as they expected it to;
- ❖ Those who have been in the market anywhere between 5 to 15 years, have grown consistently, though not spectacularly, and have now decided that it is not too late for them to become unicorns (companies with billion dollar valuations).

The courses that I offer are purchase courses typically in deemed universities around the world where I have complete ownership of the curriculum design, pedagogy and evaluation.

This experience has enhanced my own learning in an interesting way. Whilst I still shun the blatantly theoretical, jargon-based rubric, I have managed to weave a soft academic spell over my stubbornly tactile method of learning-by-doing. And I have found that this has resulted in a generous and compelling dosage of perspective to my mentees, my students and me. So, you will still find no mean theory in here, but you might find an odd reference to a not-so-mean theoretician.

Start up, Stand up! is a borrowed title. I borrowed it from Prime Minister Narendra Modi's clarion call to entrepreneurs on 15th August 2015 from the ramparts of Red Fort. *Entrepedia* was all about starting up. This book is about how to stand up once you start up, be a big boy as it were, and stand tall!

Now there is no excuse for you to say – *"I am an entrepreneur, I started up a business but I don't know how to grow it!"*

Stand up! Change the world!

And discover how changing the world looks good on you.

CONTENTS

CARMa Sutras for Growing Your Business

SUTRA I

CHOOSE YOUR FIRST
CUSTOMER CAREFULLY!

> **What would you attempt to do if you knew you could not fail?**
>
> – Robert Schuller

YOUR VALIDATED, TESTED, and maybe even piloted product is ready and you have now opened shop. You have a certain picture in your head about what your customer looks like, how he behaves and how you will engage with him. Your entire entrepreneurial journey, up until this point in time, has been focused on only one outcome: that he will pull out his wallet, count the crisp notes and smilingly hand them over to you. He will also hug you and with tears in his eyes ask: where have you been all my life?

This is the fantasy that has been playing in your head for the past year or so, ever since you started working on the idea that bamboozled you, took over your being and gobbled up your sleep. It is this one moment that you have been holding your breath for— the magical moment when you meet your first paying customer.

No words can describe it. No amount of poetry can articulate the longing, the pathos and the tingling sense of anticipation of this moment. You have lived a whole year in suspended animation just so it can culminate in this intoxicating handshake.

The truth is that your first paying customer is your biggest validation and your loftiest redemption. From concept to market, whilst product development is your first and major milestone, it is incomplete until a customer willingly walks into your parlor and asks to be seduced.

What are the things that you should keep in mind to ensure nothing goes wrong in this dream script? Here are some of the choices you need to evaluate and pick. The problem is there is no 'cut-paste' choice. What works for someone may not work for you. What fails in some business need not be a failure in your business. So, there is no formulaic answer. You have to figure out, based on your domain, idea, vision and resources, the one that works optimally for you.

Let's look at some of the choices in front of you.

Low hanging fruit or a long gestation

This is a tricky one and sometimes could be a deal-breaker. The questions that hit you could be any of the following:

Should my first customer be someone from my own network who will not require much persuasion to buy my product or should I approach a total stranger? If I go with the former, I may not get unbiased feedback and if I choose the latter I might end up expending resources rather needlessly

❖ Should I target a potential customer who is already using a similar product and just convince him to switch or should I spend my resources to find a non-user and get him to change his behavior? Switching may be simpler but will my product compare well against my competitors'? And if there is a possibility that it might not, am I not better off with a non-user?

❖ Should I drop my price so that the customer will be tempted to buy? Should I go overboard in terms of freebies just so I can boast of my first customer? Should I go with a discerning customer who appreciates the value of what I'm offering or should I simply consider purchasing power?

❖ Let's look at the example of Natural Ice-cream. There were no takers because most customers could not wrap their heads around the fact that it was natural, in that it used fresh fruits and did not have any preservatives

> Raghunandan Kamath started making and selling fresh-fruit-based ice creams in 1984, in Mumbai.

To drive footfall, Kamath started offering *Vadapaav* and other snacks. When customers flocked to him for snacks, he offered his fresh fruit ice cream free, gently persuading them to try something new. He continued with this strategy until customers came to him asking for the ice creams and not for the snacks.

Although this must have been a huge drain on his meager resources, I think Kamath realized that if you want to change user behavior, it can't be done overnight. It has to be done over time in such a way that there is a huge buy-in from the customer.

Like I said, these are questions that you need to ask yourself. There is no wrong or right answer here; it is a choice you make. But make sure it is an intelligent, calculated choice, not the one that is taken mindlessly or for the wrong reason, as it may come to bite you in the ass later.

Basic product or feature-loaded

This is a huge dilemma and I see this often in Internet products. Let's say you are developing a mobile app for dating. The app development is a long-drawn process, consuming anywhere between 120 to 250 days. Your app-developer tells you that in this time frame he can only give you a basic app, the one that allows your customers to discover each other, and to like or not like. This will cost Rs. 2.5 lakhs. If you want more sophisticated features such as ratings, testimonials, event planning, merchandising, group dating, speed dating and others, it will take 300 to 450 days. This will cost around Rs 10 lakhs.

You are likely to go with the first proposal as it is less time-consuming and fits your budget. Also, it will give you a chance to test the waters without blowing up too much of your meager resources. It should, therefore, be a straightforward choice. Except that it isn't.

Because you know that dating apps out there in the market are offering better value and more inclusive experience than yours. Hence, your basic product has lesser chances of survival. But you hesitate to choose the second option for two reasons: First, it is resource intensive. Secondly, you are concerned that by the time you hit the market in 18 months, there may be other players with deeper pockets and more innovative ideas who have blitzed the market. So what do you do?

My take is, even if you go to the market with a basic version; make sure it has a compelling value proposition for the customer. In one shot, you should be able to not only hope for a switch but also convert a non-user to a user.

Let me illustrate this with the example of mobile payment gateway. In 2010, when we were looking for payment gateway for *CARMaShala*, our online course in entrepreneurship, there were only two dominant players: Techpro and CC Avenues, both based in Mumbai. There was a third player, Oxigen, but it largely partnered with telecom service providers.

Our early interaction with both did not inspire confidence at all. Yet we went ahead with Techpro, as there were no better options. Almost up until early 2014, online payments had a failure rate of 40% and the time taken to process a transaction was 1.5 to 2 minutes. Citrus Pay, based in Mumbai, was amongst the earliest to spot an opportunity in this space. They built a robust payment gateway where the failure rate came down to 10% and transaction-processing time was down to 15-20 seconds. But they didn't just stop there. They focused on the new source of traffic coming from mobiles and added layers of analytics to their products.

This opened up the market for a number of new players such as Mobikwik and Livquik, which focused only on mobile payments. The new entrants had the option of either entering the broad spectrum of online payments or offer huge value to their customers by becoming a niche mobile payment gateway. Both chose the latter.

Build user community or monetize

This is an important decision. For example, when we launched *Chatterpillar*, our monthly digital magazine for entrepreneurs in October 2014, I was convinced we had a wonderful product in our hands and we saw no reason why we shouldn't go laughing all the way to the bank.

It is a hugely disruptive product, not just in features but also in the way we were monetizing it. Besides subscription, which was priced really low at Rs 500 for annual subscription, we had six other sources of revenue. We marketed it to our network first, which was pretty large and relevant as they were all part of the entrepreneurial ecosystem in one way or another. So the first issue not only had 10,000 subscribers but we had many takers for our job ads, company listing, product display and even pitching to investors.

For the second issue, we decided that we would approach strangers. That is when we hit a roadblock. Most people said, yes it is a good product and we like the features, but what is your subscription base? We said, "10,000 subscribers". Come back to us when your circulation increases, they would say. So, the *Chatterpillar* team had to take a call whether we should continue with its existing business model or pivot.

After several sleepless nights, we made the decision that we should pivot. We decided to first focus on building user community before monetization.

We targeted to build a subscriber base of 100,000. To be able to do that in the shortest possible time, we offered free subscription for a year. We also decided not to sell our other services until we achieved this milestone and also set a timeline. By the 31st of March, 2015 we would cross 100,000 subscribers. And till then, CARMa would fund the magazine.

By 31st March, we had only 60,000 subscribers. Not bad as a number per se, but not good considering the target we had set for ourselves. So we continued to offer free subscription.

We managed to hit that milestone only by the end of May. But by then we had also decided to offer *Chatterpillar* as a free magazine. Our revenue came from other services, which we offered with our anniversary issue in October.

My take is that, especially in B2C Internet products, putting user community ahead of monetization works wonders. See how Whatsapp benefited! At the time it was bought by Facebook, it had a user base of 450 million. All these people were using the product free and even if Whatsapp had decided to charge $1 per user a month, it was still a daunting $450 million dollars a month in revenue.

Volume or niche

Most entrepreneurs assume that branding is not important at the startup-stage and they will worry about it when the company becomes big. They have to give it primacy right from the product development stage for two reasons. One is that it helps them fence their catchment area and the other is that it helps them work on their pricing strategy.

Let me clarify something here. Being a volume player does not mean that your prices are low. Nor does being a niche player make your product a premium one. Let me give you examples to illustrate this.

Prestige pressure cookers are one of the most mass-market products. But they don't come cheap. Similarly Uber in India is a niche product company, yet its riding price is on par or even lower than that of an auto rickshaw!

It is important to be aware who you want to be before going to market so that your communication is clear. Again, there is no right or wrong choice. If you are entering a hugely disruptive market of taxis in India, you have to decide whether you want to be like Ola and Uber, whose business models depend on volume.

If you want to be in the luxury segment, operating high-end cars like Mercedes, BMW and Porsche, you would cater to a small but discerning segment of customers who need cars not for point-to-point transport but for making a statement.

A-lister or C-lister

In the B2B segment, the dilemma could be even more infuriating. If you are manufacturing gold plated printed circuit boards for watch-makers and the automotive sector, right when you are setting up the factory, you have to decide whether you will make low-end products and swamp the C-listers of both industries or very high-end premium products only for the A-listers of both industries.

This decision will impact everything, from the kind of facility you build, the talent you hire, your prices, your culture of innovation, and of course, your marketing as well as growth strategy. If you choose the A-listers, you are consciously walking towards a combination of low volume, high visibility, high margin (that holds steady in time), high investment (in the pursuit of excellence and innovation) and high risk. If you choose a C-lister, you are linking arms with a combination of high volume, low margin (that keeps eroding over time), lower capex but steadily expanding market.

Summary

Before going to market, you would have struggled and worked hard on putting a face to your customer. Once you go to market you realize that the challenge of choosing your customer is as daunting. You also realize that making the right choice with your first paying customer is as important as putting a face to your customer and has serious implications both in the short-term and long-term. Up until now, as an entrepreneur, you only obsessed about how you looked at the world. In choosing your first customer, you are taking your first tentative step towards how you want the world to see you.

TAKEAWAYS

- Getting your first paying customer is really the culmination of your entrepreneurial dream

- It is not enough that you have done your customer discovery thoroughly. You will also need to consciously pick and choose your first customer by facing and resolving choices that confront you

- The typical choices are: low hanging fruit or long gestation, volume or niche, user community or monetization, A-list customer or C-list, basic product or a feature-rich one

- Make sure you spend enough time addressing each of them so that your choices are well-thought-out and consistent with your vision

CREATE AN INNOVATIVE
BUSINESS MODEL

> ❝ **If you can't explain it to a six-year old,**
> **you don't understand it yourself** ❞
>
> – Albert Einstein

YOU NOW HAVE YOUR first paying customer. You have celebrated it with your team and before the euphoria dies down, you have to figure out how to convert one to many. This is a good time to focus on the nine building blocks of your Business Model Canvas (BMC).

Before you went to market, you had worked on many of them in a rudimentary fashion. Now is the time to firm them up. That does not mean that they are carved in stone or that you can never change them under any circumstance. All it means is now you have a little more market data to work on them and lot more confidence to stay committed to the idea along with definitive reasons to make it a success.

What is a business model? How is it different from a business plan?

> Broadly, the four areas that the BMC covers are product, customer, infrastructure and profitability.

Alexander Osterwalder, the Swiss business theorist, defines a business model as "the rationale of how an organization creates, delivers and captures value". He created the Business Model Canvas (BMC) with its nine building blocks 'to show the logic of how company intends to make money'.

Is business plan the same as business model?

Before we get down to understanding each of these nine building blocks, let me first explain how business model is different from business plan. The simplest explanation is that your BMC, which consists of nine building blocks, is nothing but key implementable elements of your business plan. In other words, if the business plan is your wish-list, your BMC is your road-map to fulfill that wish-list.

Is this whole idea of business model new? Well, both yes and no. Johannes Gutenberg in 1439 had not only invented movable-type printing but he also invented a process for mass-producing it. In putting together this process, he must have given some thought to what would be his cost of production, who his customer would be, how his customer would benefit from his product and how much he would be willing to pay for it. All of it means that he had paid attention to not only building his product but also making money from it. In other words, in as early as 15th century, Gutenberg understood the importance of BMC.

It is new in the sense that not just startups, but even large enterprises have understood the importance of BMC and have given it the primacy that it warrants. So much so, there is a framework now and it has wormed its way into the organization's gene pool. In fact, even Osterwalder's nine building blocks are more in the context of established organizations than startups. In my discussion here, I have actually modified it to suit the context of startups.

So what are these nine building blocks? Let's look at your idea logically. The starting point is an idea or concept in your head. How do you develop a concept into a full-blown business idea? The only way you can do it is by addressing the various elements that go to transform it into a business idea. What are these various elements?

Logically, the starting points are: what is my product, who is my customer and what is my value proposition to my customer so that he not only becomes my customer but also stays that way. Therefore, the first three building blocks are product, customer and value.

The reason I'm combining three of these blocks together is that one dovetails into the other – a trinity as it were. There is no product without a customer and vice versa. And there is no purpose for your product if there is no compelling differentiation or value proposition.

What comes first, product or customer?

There is an interesting sidebar to this. It is a philosophical question as to what comes first – the product or the customer. If you are an entrepreneur whose product is designed to fix a particular problem, then the customer comes first. He already has a problem and he is waiting for your product to fix it.

Customer first

A good illustration of this is Delhi-based *Chaayos*. Raghav Verma, one of the co-founders, felt that although Indians love drinking tea, there were very few places in India that served good tea, like the kind you are used to at home. Nor were there outlets that served varieties–both commonplace and exotic– for the discerning drinker. So he started Chaayos, which is well-funded and doing brisk business from several outlets today.

In this case, as I said, the customer was already there, waiting for the product.

Product first

If you are an entrepreneur creating a product first and then inducing people to use it by virtue of the disruptive nature of its value, product comes first. Let me explain this with the use case of Ola.

By aggregating existing taxis and encouraging drivers to become entrepreneurs (buy cars; get commercial registration and drive for Ola), it scaled its business in both reach and numbers quickly. Very early on, Ola realized that this was a business of volumes and the more the people use it, the more they will influence other people to use it. So they had three distinct user segments.

The first segment was people who were used to hailing taxis for work or pleasure. This was their low-hanging fruit. They would not need much persuasion to start using Ola.

The second was the people who used public transport. Here it was important to disrupt user behavior if you needed to convert them. That is exactly what Ola did. It offered fares, which were on par, or even lower, with auto-rickshaws. So in one shot it offered the convenience and style of traveling in a car but paying the same or even lesser than an auto or an AC bus.

The third segment was really the toughest. It included people who commuted only in their own cars. In India, car ownership is a status symbol and it would be really hard to convert this segment. And that's why Ola offered convenience as a value proposition.

To this customer Ola said: You don't have to drive and lose your mind in traffic, you don't have to struggle to find parking, you don't have to put up with tantrums of the driver and you don't have to pay hefty maintenance bills for your car. We will offer you the same style and comfort of your personal vehicle without all the attendant inconveniences. So Ola offered differentiated products – low-end cars for price-sensitive people and sedans for status-conscious ones.

Ola created taxi aggregation as a product but grew by inducing traditional non-users to use its product and become its customers. In this sense, the product came first.

Let's now check out the first three building blocks.

Product

Learn to define your product briefly and precisely. If your product is an app that helps you digitize, store and retrieve medical records, say so. Don't just say it is a healthcare app! I have sat through business plan pitches where at the end of the pitch I have had to ask the entrepreneur but, darling, what's your product?

When you are outlining your product, remember to include the following:

- ❖ What is my product? (app, web, media, storage, device, tool, software or platform)

- ❖ What is the technology that drives it? (In simple layman English, not techno-babble)

- ❖ Who will buy it? (B2B, B2C or B2G), and a brief description of your potential customer

- ❖ Why would he buy it ?(the tangible and intangible value that your product offers which may be in terms of features, packaging, price, channel or lifestyle). Include here a comparative chart of your and your competitors' offering to highlight how yours fares better and why, therefore, customers should flock to you

- ❖ Your cost incurred in making the product, bringing it to market and acquiring your customer

- ❖ Your price point for your product (if possible, include the rationale for the pricing)

Customer (External)

If you know how to articulate your product clearly and simply, it should be easy enough for you to say who is your customer. A good starting point is to define who is not your customer. I keep saying this – when you see a donkey on the road, you know it is a donkey and not a zebra. The typical tendency of every entrepreneur in the B2C space is to say that everyone is his customer, which is the same as saying that every four-legged creature is a donkey!

Let's take the same example of an app meant for digitizing medical records. Who is your customer? Typically, it is someone who:

- ❖ Is an internet user

- ❖ Owns a smart phone

- ❖ Accesses the internet on his smart phone
- ❖ Has someone in his immediate family who is either sick or has an illness which requires frequent medical intervention; and
- ❖ Therefore, has a plethora of medical records by way of visits to doctors, their comments, lab reports, prescriptions and the like
- ❖ Would like to manage them in such a way that they are easy to store, retrieve and use

In other words, he needs an app that does all of this in a digital format.

The world has a population of 6.4 billion. Does every one of them qualify as your customer in the manner described above? Most certainly not, as you will agree. Less than 1% of the global population qualifies.

So everyone is not your customer!

Customer (Internal)

You should also include here your internal customer, that is, your management team. It is good to have an organogram for the next three years that will depict your entire team structure. Teams are typically classified into three categories.

The first is the founding team; the entrepreneurs who conceived of the idea and came together to implement it. They are also the owners of equity.

The second is the hired team. They are the people whom you recruit for various functions, with a clear delineation of roles, responsibility and compensation.

The third is the advisory board, which you may set up for the value that they bring to the table in terms of their brand equity, network and knowledge.

Value

Your value statement is nothing but your seduction style. You are wooing your customer – music, candles, ambience and poetry – the whole nine yards – by telling him how you have created a brilliant product and how it will make his life way better. It is your first moment of truth.

Once you have defined your product and put a face to your customer, you know clearly the value you have created. Now you have to focus on communicating that value, clearly and simply, to him. It doesn't stop there. Once you communicate, you have to make sure that you deliver that value without fail.

When you create value, communicate value and deliver value, you have achieved your purpose of becoming an entrepreneur.

In the BMC, the next sets of building blocks are strategy, partnerships and innovation.

Strategy

If business plan is your treasure chest, then strategy is the key that unlocks it. Strategy is a composite of all the logical activities that you need to engage in to make sure that you have the right key. I am using the word, composite, because it involves all aspects of your business. Not only that, in each aspect of the business, there are strategies for different purposes. Check this out!

❖   There is a customer facing strategy, which defines how you should behave when you are interacting with your customer

- There is a customer acquisition strategy, which articulates where you are likely to find your customer and how you should communicate with him to make him your customer

- There is a customer engagement strategy, which is, once you have acquired your customer, how do you keep him so happy that he gets you other customers

- Similarly, strategy can be in the area of financial discipline (or how not to splurge after being funded)

- You could have a clear recruitment strategy too. Typically, when you are in the pre-capital stage, your strategy is to hire people who come free or cheap, like interns or freshers. But when you get funded, your strategy changes to get the best talent money can buy

- You can and should have an innovation strategy that will help you foster a culture in your organization that is curious, nimble-footed and completely tuned to disrupting user behavior

Basically, all the strategies have one purpose only – to help your organization grow from one paying customer to many.

Partnerships

This refers to all your outsourced relationships. Your partners could be in the area of technology, channel, marketing, finance or accounts. For example, you may outsource your accounts to a chartered accountancy firm. You could partner with a digital media agency to manage your digital footprint. Similarly, you could sell your product through a distributor network or third party ecommerce sites, or you could partner with a technology company to create and manage your dynamic portal, app development and the like.

In today's age, partnerships are crucial on three counts. First, you don't have to reinvent the wheel. If someone has already created a piece of the business that is useful to you, you simply make use of it under a Memorandum of Understanding (MoU). Since it is not humanly possible to know everything about everything, it makes sense to partner with someone whose domain it is. This means you won't be wasting time, effort and money.

Secondly, it is much easier to hold partners accountable under the MoU than employees. I have seen this at close quarters. One of my mentees insisted on hiring coders for his product development. After three years and five team changes, the product is still languishing and is nowhere near market-ready.

Thirdly, partners bring their own network too and that is hugely important for an entrepreneur. This could be by way of customers, service providers and team members.

Innovation

There are typically two kinds of innovation. Those that you have thought through in the pre-market stage as part of your product development and those you got on board, after going to market, either based on customer feedback or spotting an opportunity in your ecosystem. Let me give you examples of both.

In 2007, when Sachin Bansal and Binny Bansal started Flipkart, the first and only product they offered was books. The other categories that they eventually added such as electronics, fashion, lifestyle, etc., must have been in their innovation pipeline. An assorted basket of products in multiple categories meant wider catchment area, more footfalls, more conversions and better averaging out of margins. Right at the time when they were ideating, in the pre-market stage, they must have had their GANTT chart in place – what categories, what range of products in these categories and what timelines. This is a typical example of innovation in the pre-market stage (Flipkart has since discontinued this).

The second kind of innovation is based on customer feedback and evolving dynamics of the marketplace. For example, being in the market for a decade now and also a leader in it, Flipkart is constantly trying to bridge the gap between online and offline shopping in India by using data analytics. To this end, they launched Ping which is a chat messenger inside the app where customers can engage in a live conversation with friends to make the best buying decision. How does Ping work?

Let's say you are in a shopping mall and a girl walks in wearing a dress that instantly makes your eyes light up. You could take a picture of this dress and pop up all such similar dresses available on Flipkart on your app. Not only that, you can share the images with friends and ask them which one suits you the most! Obviously, when Flipkart started in 2007, they had not come up with this product in their innovation pipeline. As big data gathers momentum and as Flipkart positions itself to deploy technology across the board to enable a robust ecommerce in India, such innovations are spawned by the dynamics of the emerging marketplace.

The last three building blocks on the BMC grid are channel, monetization and branding.

Channel

This refers to the platform on which the customer can access your products. So what are the typical options in today's world?

Your product may be available only in a physical store. It could be in a retail outlet, it could be in a hospital or a gym, it could be a kiosk outside a shopping mall or it could be a dispenser in a corporate office. The retail outlet could be your own exclusive store or a franchise or you could populate the shelves of multi-brand stores. For example, Fabindia. Their products are sold through their own stores. They opened their first store in 1976 in New Delhi. Since then, they have grown to 189 outlets throughout India and about 10 stores overseas. They also sell online, but my guess is their in-store business is way more than their online sales.

Your product could be online on web. It could be on your own portal or on other product portals, or you could even have your own online store on eBay. NDTV Ethnics, for instance, is an online portal for traditional ethnic fashion apparel, promoted by Prannoy Roy and his wife Radhika Roy, to give market access to designer craftsmen. It sells premium products designed by master craftsmen from across the country.

Your product could be on social media. I have a mentee who runs a company called 'Steal a Style' where she sells all her designer *ghagra cholis* on Facebook.

Your channel may be a hybrid one in the sense that your products are available both online and offline. Decathlon, for instance, sells everything connected with all kinds of adventure sports, and sells it all through massive retail outlets as well as online on www.decathlon.in

You could also be selling your product on the phone. The best example I can think of is phone-sex. The 1-888-395-5412 number heralded a whole new industry and caught the imagination of the populace largely because you can be as vicarious as you choose, but hidden behind the comfort and anonymity of your phone.

The last of the channel options is MLM or multi-level marketing. This is a concept popularized by companies such as Tupperware,

Amway, Modicare and the like. The business model here is once you become a customer, you are recruited to be a salesperson too. The layers are built in a pyramidal hierarchy and everyone in that hierarchy earns for every sale but in different percentages depending on where you are in that hierarchy.

Monetization

This is perhaps the most important building block in your BMC. You may have an excellent product but if you haven't identified various ways of making money from your business, you will fall by the wayside soon. It is important that you identify at least five different streams of revenue.

The typical options for monetizing, especially in new age businesses are as vast as your imagination. For example, let us say your product is a Harley Davidson bikers' club. This may be an online community. The primary requisite for membership is that you should be a proud owner of an HD bike. The monetization avenues may be as follows:

❖ Subscription – For example, a fee may be charged to become a member of this club. The fee may be in the form of an annual subscription that gives you free access to checking out member profiles, monthly newsletters and you may also get preferential treatment and discount at HD events all over the world

❖ Value-added services (VAS) – There may be some free basic services but for any add-on service, you may be charged a premium. For example, you may be able to chat with other members online, exchange stories, post pictures etc. absolutely free, but you may be charged a fee if you want to participate in an HD rally

❖ Co-branding/affiliate membership – The club may have an

affiliate partnership with let's say Patagonia or Decathlon. So any of the biking equipment and apparel that you buy from either of these may be at a very attractive discount on producing a membership card of the bikers' club

❖ Advertising – This is the tried and tested source of revenue. For instance, Wildcraft, which sells backpacks, rucksacks and shoes, may advertise on your portal and app because both of you have common customers

❖ Analytics – In today's parlance, this is a big-ticket item. Most of the capital deployment by ecommerce companies is in the area of using technology to understand user behavior, not only as closely as possible but in real time. So Ping, which is a tool that bridges the online-offline gap for Flipkart's customers, is looking to add a shopping assistant, quite like Siri, to understand not only what the customer wants but predict his behavior with a fair amount of accuracy

Branding

The last building block in this grid is branding. Every entrepreneur believes that in the first few years of his business, his unwavering focus should be on building his product and selling it. If you were to ask him about branding, his typical reply will be 'I will worry about it when the company becomes big'.

Nothing could be a bigger mistake than this. It may come as a surprise to many when I say that branding is an exercise which you have to focus on pretty much from Day Zero.

Branding is the persona that you create of your business. You have to know if your business is a Maruti 800 or a Ferrari! You have to remember that you are your brand's biggest, most evangelical and most memorable ambassador. Customers and employees alike love many new age brands today for the charisma of their CEO's who are also their brand ambassadors.. In a recent survey conducted by the US-based Glassdoor.com, both Shashank N.D of Practo and Sachin Bansal of Flipkart have emerged as CEOs with the highest approval ratings from their employees (100 percent and 94 percent respectively).

Summary

The nine building blocks of your BMC are important, not only because they help you think through all aspects of your business but also because it is a good intellectual exercise where you create the blueprint for your company. Suddenly what was just an erratic concept or notion in your head acquires legitimacy and allows you to forge ahead, fearlessly.

TAKEAWAYS

- The BMC is an excellent reference tool for you to create a roadmap for all aspects of your business, logically, coherently and consistenly
- It gives you the freedom to ideate, pivot, and reinvent, almost on the fly
- It should be treated as a work-in-progress document and as an entrepreneur, you should keep visiting it to review it, tweak it and update it
- It is an excellent risk-mitigation tool

SUTRA III

HOW DO YOU ACQUIRE YOUR CUSTOMERS?

> ❝ **People don't care how much you know
> until they know how much you care** ❞
>
> – Theodore Roosevelt

CONTRARY TO WHAT MOST entrepreneurs believe that the starting point of all entrepreneurial journeys is an *'idea'*, (this is a fact, not a baseless generalization, considering that there are even books about how idea is the starting point), it is actually the customer, the person whose life the idea purports to affect. Many decades ago, even before technology brought the world together on a single platform, Peter Drucker said, 'the purpose of a business is to create and keep a customer'.

Take Apple iPod, for instance. I am sure Steve Jobs did not tell his design team: guys let's develop a fantastic technology to listen to music and then we will go find a customer. It was more like, how can we make listening to music easy (music on-the-go) and fun (a personalized playlist)? Also, not to just listen to whatever music companies compile and sell but be able to search and buy individual pieces of music that I like from one place (that's how iTunes Store was born). Once they decided on this, they created the product. Eventually the iPod not only revolutionized the way we listen to music but disrupted the whole industry.

But the travesty is that rarely do entrepreneurs recognize this. For them, it is always the product that consumes their energy and drives all other activities. The idea originated because they wanted to change human behavior, yet nary a thought was given to this animal called customer! I go through 60 business plans a week. I have been doing so for over a decade now. Never once have I come across an entrepreneur who starts out by making his customer central to his entrepreneurial theme. Not even when he is addressing the pain point of a section of people or a gap in the market.

For instance, let's say, an entrepreneur is designing software, which regulates traffic flow. He sees the people whom it will positively affect, as a nebulous collective, PEOPLE. Ask him who these people are, ask him to put a face to this collective, and he will shrug his shoulders and say, all those who are traveling and are stuck in traffic!

My guess is that this product obsession to the exclusion of everything else stems from the simplistic notion that if I put out a kickass product in the market place, customers will queue up on their own, magnetized by my product.

I don't know if this is rank naiveté on their part or they are willfully oblivious to the fact that a product cannot exist in a vacuum. In fact, it doesn't even qualify as a product unless there is a customer for it – a product and its customer are the two sides of the same coin.

After a decade of teaching and mentoring, I have realized that there are two kinds of entrepreneurs – those that set out to make lives better by fixing an existing problem with a solution and those that seek a solution, even without a stated problem. Both are do-gooders. Both want to make people's lives better.

What is common between the two is that both believe everyone is their customer! To my mind, this ridiculously blinkered approach is what makes startups so vulnerable and causes 90% mortality in the first year of going to market.

So let's start from the beginning. The question 'how do I acquire my customer' presupposes three things:

- ❖ Who is my customer?
- ❖ Where will I find him?
- ❖ How will I bring him home (make him my customer)?

Let us examine each of these questions. To understand these three questions better, let us take the use-case of UrbanClap.

(Disclaimer: I am not claiming that this is how UrbanClap did its customer discovery. I am just using UrbanClap as an example to walk readers through the process of customer discovery)

Who is my customer?

UrbanClap was founded by two batch mates at IIT Kanpur, Varun Khaitan and Abhiraj Bhal. A third, Raghav Chandra, came on board after they met him through some mutual friends.

It is not that they were the first to come up with this idea or the only ones. There are others like Doormint, TimeSaverz, Taskbob, Mr.Right and Zepper.

UrbanClap is a mobile platform that fulfills typical urban needs such as the need for a carpenter, a wedding planner or even a masseuse. The services are delivered in the convenience of your home or workspace.

What grabbed my imagination was the explanation put out by the co-founders as to why they called it UrbanClap. They said, *Urban* because we are focusing on the unmet needs of people living in urban areas and *Clap* because every time we meet the needs of these customers, they should applaud our service.

Now that is what I call an excellent product design; one that attracts customers by virtue of its inherent empathy for them. Not by shouting from rooftops that such a service is available. It also beautifully illustrates my point that the entrepreneurial journey begins, not with an idea, but with a customer.

UrbanClap is very clear about who its customers are. They are people:

❖ Who live and work in cities

❖ Whose dining table needs a carpenter to fix its glass top

❖ Who need a beautician at home on the weekend for a facial to chase the week's blues away (it is just so much more relaxing at home!)

❖ Who want a driver to take them for a wedding (who wants to drive and let the bad traffic spoil the mood?); and

❖ Who require a wedding photographer for their parents' golden wedding anniversary (someone who would capture those splendid emotional moments as candidly as possible)

Although the customers are both men and women, I do believe that UrbanClap has made the lives of women much easier because it is they who are responsible for upkeep and maintenance of their homes and have an almost obsessive need to have everything in working condition, as many empirical studies have shown. These are men and women who:

❖ Earn well as professionals (family income of over Rs. 25 lakhs per annum)

❖ Are married with one or two kids (in the age group of 4 to 10 years)

❖ Live mostly in nuclear units but have strong bonds with their own parents

❖ Travel overseas regularly for work

❖ Are quite house-proud as they live in their own homes (although some may have company-rented apartments), and also often entertain guests at home

❖ Mostly live in apartments (this varies from city to city. In Gurgaon and Mumbai it will be only apartments and in Bangalore, Hyderabad and Chennai, it may include independent houses where it is even harder to find someone to fix things)

❖ Who are brand conscious (and who shop in flea markets only when they go abroad)

❖ Dress trendy and own two cars, one a sedan, maybe a Maruti SX4–which is also the family car–and the other, a smaller one, maybe a Swift

❖ Who enjoy socializing and love watching movies on weekends at multiplexes

❖ Who take at least one big vacation and two small vacations a year

❖ Who enjoy eating at a fine dining restaurant at least once a month

❖ Who love to try out new restaurants in town

❖ Who believe that *Chaat* is the best street food

❖ Who regularly shop online for groceries, clothes, home décor, furniture and the like

Observe carefully the demographic profile that I have drawn above and you will see that it has not been put together randomly. There is almost a subtle deductive process involved here. It is a scientific process of extrapolation that is used regularly in market research.

For example, by and large you begin to own a lot of things in an apartment only when you are a family. Chances are that both husband and wife are working and therefore do not have the time to have things fixed when they break down. They have the disposable income that supports a good lifestyle. Since they also travel abroad on work, they have exposure to lifestyles and products. The rest follows.

So who is UrbanClap's customer? If you were to put a face to UrbanClap's customer on the basis of the profiling we have just done, what would it be like in a nutshell?

Couples in the age group of 28 to 40, living in cities, who studied engineering and are working in large IT organizations, with a good disposable income, who change their smart phones every year because they pretty much manage their lives on their phones, are willing to pay for the convenience of having a well-run home and who want to enjoy the good life because that is what they are earning for.

If you are generally idling outside a shopping mall and you want to amuse yourself, will you be able to say, with certainty, looking at the crowd around you, who is UrbanClap's customer and who is not, based on the above profile? You bet you can!

When you are addressing the question – who is my customer – remember two things. The first is that customer discovery is a bell-shaped curve. 60% of your customers fall under the bell. And

20% each fall on either side of the bell. When you are identifying your customer, you are identifying only the 60% that fall under the bell because bulk of your revenues comes from them. The 20% on either side are your potential group for the future, you may have to tweak your product to get them under the bell but for the moment, either because they are not regular buyers or they are non-buyers, you will steer clear of them.

The second is that it is a good exercise that will serve as the starting point to identifying who is not your customer. I don't mean that you simply write the opposite of everything you have used in profiling. But if UrbanClap were to put a face to its non-customer, it would be something like this:

❖ Couples living in rented homes or parental property

❖ In joint families

❖ Whose idea of entertainment is going to Big Bazaar on republic day as a family

❖ More focused on home as a tidy, hygienic place than an aesthetically laid out space

❖ Use low-end mobile phones and even if they do splurge Rs 10,000 on a Micromax, used largely for calls and SMS and shooting family pictures on the camera and less for the internet

❖ Own a Bajaj scooter

❖ Husband works in a private company in a middle management position, maybe in accounts or administration

❖ Wife is either a home-maker or a school teacher

❖ Two kids aged between 4 and 8, studying in the same school where their mother probably teaches

❖ When anything needs to be fixed at home, the husband

does it or they call the neighborhood handyman, haggle with him over price and take the delay and not-so-great quality of execution in their stride

❖ Joint family income of Rs 6-8 lakhs

❖ Avid TV watchers, in fact dinner is usually in front of the TV while watching a regional (their mother tongue or Hindi) soap

❖ Buy clothes for the whole family, once a year, during *Diwali*

So the face that emerges from this profiling is of

> A couple who have strong 'saving' values so that they can provide good-quality education to their children who, when they grow up, will look after them and provide a greater degree of comfort than they themselves could afford, while the children were growing up.

This exercise is very important. I always say this, if you see a dog on the road, you know it is a dog and not a camel. How do you know that? You know it, not only because of its features and characteristics, but you also know that whilst dogs are plentiful on the roads, camels are unlikely fixtures on urban landscapes!

Like I said, this category could, over time, become part of the catchment area but not at the moment.

Where will I find him?

Once you have profiled who your customer is and who your customer is not, the next step is to figure out the most likely places to find him. So a good starting point again is to avoid those places where your non-customer is likely to be. Let me explain.

In my profiling of UrbanClap's customer, I have said that he is the one who works in large IT organizations. So that's your low hanging fruit. Go find him there. You can reach him in his office. Don't look for him in places you don't expect him to be.

The best way of access is by identifying him in your own network through all the people who work in IT organizations. Reach out to them. Tell them about the UrbanClap mobile app and what it does. Ask them to download the app and share among their friends.

Find more IT people from your LinkedIn network. Reach out to them. Send invitation to more people on LinkedIn, working in IT companies. Incentivize them to download the app, and tell their friends about it. Also introduce a referral discount. And before you say Jack Robinson, some hundred people have downloaded the app. Your first few paying customers have to, necessarily, come from your own network.

Then you try and find out where he lives. Figure out all the upscale apartments typically occupied by IT professionals. Avoid MIG (Middle Income Group) flats or small independent dwellings in the old part of the city (non-customer).

Talk to the secretary of the residents' association; pay some money to have a small printed handout dropped into their mailboxes. On a Sunday, set up a kiosk in the apartment complex (again you will have to pay to the association) for a couple of hours. Put up some display banners inviting the residents to meet with you. Talk to them about the relevance of UrbanClap in their life. Explain to them that most apartment complexes offer maintenance support by way of electrician and plumber but if you need a carpenter or painter or masseuse, it is a Herculean task to get one. Simultaneously use the power of social media. Create interesting mailers using MailChimp. Send it out to people in your network and ask them to share it with their friends. Maybe, even put it out on their company intranet.

Please remember that when you use social media, you have to define the purpose clearly and accordingly choose content. In the early days, it is all about creating awareness of how UrbanClap can address their pain point. Don't be disappointed if conversions don't happen immediately. If you are smart, you will use personalized content, not some random posts, to get them interested in you. Run campaigns. Incentivize. Be inventive. Use animation. Use graphics. Get potential customers to talk about their pain points.

Once conversions begin to happen, change the message. Talk about your customers and their happy experiences like how hard they clapped. Please remember that it is your responsibility as an entrepreneur to ensure, firstly, that you acquire the customer and having acquired him/her to make doubly sure that he/she claps!

UrbanClap was founded in November 2014 and in the first couple of months, there were about 50 to 70 customers a day. Today, that number has risen to about 2500 a day. At that time, they had about 300 service providers. Today they have over 5000. This Gurgaon-based company has expanded to 10 cities in less than six months.

How will I bring him home?

You have profiled your customer. You know where to find him. Half the battle is already won. Now all that remains is for people to use your services and applaud you the way you want them to. Then the message goes viral. That is when your product-design wins you customers.

What can you say to your customer to make him use your product?

In the beginning, most of your conversations are with people known to you. So they will come on board without much persuasion. Once they use your services, if they feel like the proverbial cat that swallowed the canary, they will not only clap, but they will tell anyone who cares to listen.

This is a crucial stage where your product design should be such that there is not an element of discord from the time of downloading the app to service fulfilment. The User Interface (UI) should be seamless, every screen should have a call-to-action button that can be easily spotted; booking a service should be highly intuitive and service delivery should be flawless. It is said that good quality is when customer comes back to you, not the product. Your whole effort should be in making the entire process a simple, convenient, smooth and compelling experience for the customer.

Let me explain this with my own experience with UrbanClap and how I became its evangelical customer.

A couple of months ago I went to Bangalore. When I was heading home from the airport, I heard an advertisement of UrbanClap on the radio. When I reached home, I downloaded the app on my mobile. I wanted a carpenter. And there I encountered my first 'Wow!' moment.

The screen asked me what was the kind of work that I wanted the carpenter to do and it gave me some very useful options such as fixing broken furniture, getting new furniture made and interiors. I said interiors (I wanted to change the wooden flooring in a small area in my drawing room). Then it asked me when I wanted the carpenter to visit – day and time with options. I simply had to tick against the one that suited me. I chose the next day, 11 am.

At 10.50, the next morning, I got a call from the carpenter that he was reaching my place in ten minutes. He turned out to be a portly North Indian who spoke *Kannada* fairly well on account of being in Bangalore for about 8 years. I told him what I wanted. I also told him that since I don't live in Bangalore, I needed this job to be done by the following day.

He gave me a quote that included both material and labor. I thought it was a little on the higher side but nothing alarming. He promptly went out and brought me the design cards (actually he brought me several albums), gently guided me to choose one design and asked for 100% advance.

I hesitated. I asked him if I could pay once the job was complete. He said you have to pay at least the cost of the material upfront. I said, I don't know you and how would I know you will turn up tomorrow. He said, well you have to trust me. I did and paid him.

Then I called up the call center of UrbanClap in Gurgaon. A pleasant guy picked up my call almost immediately (no irritating IVR prompts). I told him that I was using UrbanClap for the first time, so I wanted to know if the carpenter was genuine as I had paid him in advance. He immediately confirmed that it was indeed their man and I had nothing to worry about. That was my second 'Wow!' moment.

The carpenter was to come home the next day at 9.30 am. He came at 9 am, with an assistant. Without wasting a minute and without messing around at all, they both completed the work by 3 pm. They collected the balance and left. That was my third and by far the biggest 'Wow!' moment!

It didn't just stop there. The next evening, the same guy from the call center called and asked if I was happy with the work. I didn't just clap. I gave UrbanClap a thunderclap! (pun on the word, Thunderclap is also a social media platform to mobilize crowd cheering)

Since then, I have talked about UrbanClap to everyone. And I mean EVERYONE! Not just this, I even went to the extent of telling people that when I retire, I would like to come back to Bangalore because UrbanClap is there that will make my life easy!

So how did UrbanClap take me home? With sheer product design! Remember, as Steve Jobs said, design is not what it looks, but what it does

Has UrbanClap taken me home just once? No way. I have used their services only once so far because I haven't been to Bangalore since and unfortunately they don't operate in Goa (and I keep telling them that they should). But they have my complete mindshare and I'm sure I will go back to them whenever I have a need.

One of the myths of customer acquisition is that once you acquire a customer you should constantly keep him engaged because out-of-sight is out-of-mind, apparently! Usually, it means bombarding the customer's mailbox with updates and announcements and irritating the hell out of him. UrbanClap hasn't done any of that. Instead, the experience they designed for me was so compelling that I'm continuously engaged with them!

When you have an excellent product design like UrbanClap, your customer becomes your most evangelical salesman and gets you more customers. So your own cost of customer acquisition stays low! I honestly can't think of anything more of a win-win situation than this!

Summary

I hope this use-case of UrbanClap has given you more than just an idea of how to acquire your customers. Irrespective of what your product is, if you show people the relevance of your product, not with arrogance (not 'I'm god's gift to mankind') but with empathy (show that you care), you will be like the 'Pied Piper' with a huge fan following! Every collateral that you use, every message that you put out and every action that you engage in should reiterate empathy, both consistently and gently.

TAKEAWAYS

- It is not enough to be product-centric as an entrepreneur. You need to be customer-obsessed

- Don't assume that if you put out a good product, there will be a line-up of customers on your doorstep. It rarely happens, may be except when it comes to life-saving drugs, or may be not even then

- Before setting out to acquire your customer, profile him thoroughly

- Once you acquire him, keep him so seduced through a compelling user experience, that he acquires other customers for you

SUTRA IV

FIND A MENTOR FOR
YOURSELF

> **The greatest good you can do for another is not just to share your riches but to reveal to them *their* own**
>
> – Benjamin Disraeli

HERE I WILL FOCUS on what kinds of mentors you need at different stages in the life of your organization and why you need them.

Who is a mentor? In India, the term has always been used randomly and anybody who gives you advice is a mentor. By that logic, in India, everybody is everybody's mentor because everybody loves giving everybody else unsolicited advice!

In the context of entrepreneurship, a mentor is someone who will, as should be evident, bring his knowledge, skill and network to the table. That is a given. But a great mentor is someone who treats mentoring as a two-way street. The more he mentors, the more he learns and it is this attitude that makes a huge difference to the mentee.

I have heard from senior management professionals that they want to mentor because they want to 'give back to society'. I find that strange. Effectively, what they are saying is that they are like Santa Claus with a bag of Christmas goodies, looking for charity cases. That attitude sucks. In the last decade of mentoring, I have found that mentoring affords the mentor a huge opportunity to learn and that is the reason why someone should want to become a mentor!

So as a mentor, my attitude is typically this: I am not God. I know a little, and you, my dear mentee, know a little. Together, during the process of mentoring, let us learn much more. In CARMa, we have mentored over 2000 entrepreneurs from 300 + domains. It is not that we were experts in every domain. We knew some, but we learnt a lot more during the process of mentoring. Our mentees brought their knowledge to the table, as did other domain experts whom we brought in for mentoring conversations. And together, we all went home significantly enriched. Honestly, this is the most exciting part of mentoring that your learning curve remains seriously northward!

Considering that we give primacy to the attitude of the mentor, not everybody with over 10 years of corporate experience qualifies as a good mentor. Conversely, anyone who has the attitude of 'mentoring-is-all-about-learning' can be an excellent mentor even if he has less than 5 years of experience. Having said this, I must qualify my statement.

In CARMa, we have classified mentors as product/domain specialists and organizational experts. In the former, mentoring is typically from an industry leader in that domain. It could be food processing, electronics, software or mobile app. Here, as long as they are au courant with the latest technology and trends in that domain, being young is not a barrier at all.

However, when it comes to organizational mentoring which is all about building the business around the idea such as getting the product market-ready, hiring talent, mobilizing user community, pricing, creating legal and statutory framework, and of course, managing resources, the organization-building experience of the mentor is very important. So we typically bring on board senior corporate professionals who have had long stints as strategic business unit (SBU) heads and have built not only their verticals but have contributed significantly for the growth of their organization.

The interesting thing is, as an entrepreneur, you need different kinds of mentors at different stages in the life cycle of your organization. Let s look at all of them.

Pre-market

In the pre-market phase, you need a mentor who can help you build a robust and value-enriched product, do your customer discovery without any ambiguity, create a legal framework to your business and in essence, help you create the Business Model Canvas, even if a tad sketchily. The mentor needs to have a good understanding of your product, its potential value proposition and its logical customer profile. The network he brings to the table at this stage may be in the areas of technology, market research, statutory and legal obligations and contracts. Basically, you need someone with the skill-set of getting you market-ready, which means, someone who can help you visualize the commercialization of a business idea that was once just a concept in your head.

Post-market

But once you go to market, you need a mentor to help you firm up your Business Model Canvas into a blueprint that you can implement. This is where the gray hair of your mentor comes in handy. In the pre-market stage, you were only ideating on paper all the what-if scenarios. Now that you have gone to market, you will be testing not only your product but also all the assumptions you made when you created your Business Model Canvas. So your mentor should be able to help you in this process of validation, on the fly! And believe me, there are so many googlies that can take you by complete surprise. Let's look at some typical scenarios:

- ❖ The customer may think your product is too basic
- ❖ He may think it is so feature-rich that it is actually confusing!
- ❖ If you are offering it free, he may try the first time around but may not continue because he thinks there is a catch somewhere
- ❖ You may have seriously worked on the user interface (UI) to make it as seamless as possible, but your customer thinks it sucks
- ❖ The customer may prefer your web interface to your app as he is more comfortable working on a larger device than a handheld phone
- ❖ The customer may use the product in a manner that you never intended. For example, Unilever used to have a detergent soap called Sunlight and it was a huge hit with women in rural India as an excellent shampoo!
- ❖ Your customer may not understand your value proposition, so he may dismiss you as a 'me too', that is, nothing unique, and stay away from it

Any of these will have you scurrying back to the drawing board. The biggest one, of course, is that you may realize, after hitting the market that you made a serious blunder in customer discovery and the person you thought was your customer was not your customer at all! A mentor by your side in such times is not only for helping you rejig your product and go-to-market strategy but also in making sure that you don't fall apart.

Pivot

The dictionary definition of 'pivot', amongst other things, is 'whirling about on one foot'. In other words, it means being lithe and nimble. It is a beautiful word in entrepreneurship as many a time it decides whether an entrepreneur is successful or not. It refers not just to the entrepreneur's nimble-footedness but also his ability to read the situation that warrants it. It has to be on point - the precision of the pirouette of a ballet dancer- not a minute too soon or too late.

For example, you may launch packaged sugarcane juice in interior Maharashtra. People are buying here and there but the product is not flying off the shelf as you expected. A few conversations with your prospective customers tell you that typical Maharashtrians are used to flavored sugarcane juice from the local *thelawalla* (hand-cart seller) who spikes it with either lemon or kokum and sprinkles salt and pepper before serving. As a result, the locals have forgotten the plain taste of sugarcane juice.

Now you may say, well since they have forgotten, my product will remind them the taste of it, so you stay with your basic product. Or you may say, if my customer wants flavored sugarcane juice, then who am I to say no? So you may pivot to offer flavored sugarcane juice. You may price it a tad higher than the *thelawalla* as you have an unassailable value proposition in terms of hygiene and shelf life. And you may go a step further and add new flavors, maybe, Mahua.

You may pivot before going to market or after going to market. This is where a mentor is most useful. He is not only keenly watching the expression on the faces of your audience but his antenna is hyper-sensitive to even a yawn or a shuffle in the seat or a sigh. The moment he feels that the audience is getting bored, before they start throwing eggs at you, he is able to pull you aside and give you some fresh lines, which might put the zing back into your act. I don't know whether Kunal Bahl of Snapdeal ever had a mentor but what I do know is that he pivoted six times in four years! From a daily deals platform in 2010 that was inspired by Groupon, even as it was exiting India at that time, Snapdeal morphed into an online marketplace in less than 15 months.

In other words, you pivot in either of the following two scenarios. The first is when your product is not being accepted as it is and the market is clearly indicating that it needs to be tweaked.

The second scenario is even more interesting and disruptive. Your product may be doing reasonably well but you see a bigger opportunity either in something altogether new or connected with it. You make the bold decision to withdraw your product, go back to the drawing board and come back with the new product to disrupt the market. That is exactly what Inmobi did and I do believe that Naveen Tiwari would not have built it into this amazing company, if he and his team had not pivoted.

Pulse on the Ecology

Another important area where a mentor is necessary is to keep you abreast of changes in government policies. As an entrepreneur, you are way too immersed in the rigor of building your business. You have an eye on what is immediately relevant to your business such as your competitor's antics in the marketplace but you might have missed out an announcement by the government that may impact your business.

For example, in 2014, in the wake of the Uber episode, where one of their drivers had allegedly raped a woman in Delhi, the Delhi government announced that even taxi-apps come under the radio-taxi category and therefore should be allowed to operate only after obtaining a license. This put Ola, Uber and the other similar businesses in jeopardy. My guess is that if both of them had a mentor he would have flagged this as a distinct possibility early on.

Getting you investment-ready

Investment is another area where mentors play a crucial role. Typically, as the business grows, the entrepreneur gets sucked into its vortex. When this happens, the biggest casualties are financial discipline, customer conversations and team management, not in any particular order. The standard excuse as to why no processes and systems are in place is that "oh, we grew too fast, where was the time, we just did everything on the go".

Doing things on the go is a wonderful thing because it demonstrates your ability to think on your feet but it can't be in an anarchical way. It has to be within the framework of 'do's and don'ts'. Else, it can be an exhausting process for everyone concerned and the cracks will appear very soon. Creating standard operating procedures (SoP's) for every major activity within the organization is a non-negotiable imperative and this is where mentors can be extremely useful.

In 2012, a middle-aged entrepreneur approached us for mentoring. He said he, along with his three co-founders, wanted mentoring to manage their company's growth. In the last three years, their company had grown 500% annually. They had multiple swanky offices including one in the Middle East. Each of the four co-founders took home a fancy package. They traveled executive class, stayed only in five-star hotels and entertained their customers in style. There always seemed to be enough money in the company to support their expansive style of management.

Then they bought a company in Kuwait in an all-cash deal. The CFO who was a hired employee expressed his concern a few times, saying that the asking price was probably way too much and their books of accounts seemed to be dodgy. But the founders convinced their Board that this was a good buy which would take them into the big league right away and if they had to grow organically, it would take them at least three more years to get there. They bought the company.

And then the proverbial shit hit the proverbial fan. As the CFO suspected, the accounts had been given a huge make-over. There were litigations in seven countries from large customers and vendors. The promoters had raided all the assets of the company and had pretty much sold them an empty shell for a whopping price.

Of course, our mentee had not told us any of these things at the time he approached us. All he had said was this: "We have bought this amazing business in the Middle East. We want to be able to integrate it well into our company and leverage the strengths for an exponential growth. So mentor us".

By the time we got on the second mentoring call, we knew something stank. Then I had a conversation with the CFO and got the whole story.

Finally, after a lot of dredging, what emerged was that whilst the company had grown fast and furious, the processes and systems that were to lend the right framework had never been put in place. Every time, they invented processes as the situation demanded. Sometimes it worked, often it didn't. But no one even paused to review what was working and what was not.

They did the same thing in evaluating the business they were looking to acquire. After two meetings and five emails, the decision was made to buy at the price as quoted. Even the CFO's concerns were brushed aside. The excuse: "Oh, we were growing so fast. Where was the time for a detailed due diligence?"

I sat with the founding team and told them that if they wanted us to mentor them they would have to prepare themselves for a brutal restructuring on every single front. This would involve downsizing the team, shutting down a couple of offices, moving into a basic work space, ruthlessly cutting short their losses on bad investments and managing their resources with surgical frugality. I also told them that, in the process, there was a distinct possibility that they may lose some customers. If they were prepared for all of this, I said, we would continue to mentor them. If not, we would discontinue mentoring. After much internal discussion, they decided to shut shop and absorb the losses to move on. The last time I heard, all four of them had gone back to the IT multinational company they had come from.

Becoming investment ready is the process of demonstrating a credible business model canvas; a scalable, feasible and profitable business plan to weave it all into a compelling story that entices the investor in having an important part written for him. Right now it is a very one-sided relationship. The entrepreneur is expected only to pitch his executive summary or synopsis to the investor and the investor is expected to be a visionary who can add as many zeroes to the top line as his imagination allows him to.

In reality, the entrepreneur is the scriptwriter; he may change a dialogue here and there to accommodate the investor, but the story belongs to him as do the characters. The investor is only one of the characters.

Interestingly, apart from the above-mentioned reasons, I have found that entrepreneurs approach mentors for the following reasons:

1. To write a business plan

At a concept stage, many entrepreneurs approach us because they expect us to write the business plan for them! It has taken me ten long years to impress upon them that if the idea is theirs, **they** have to write the business plan and not me. A mentor's role is to get them to flesh out in as much detail as possible– each of the nine building blocks– so that they can all come together logically to form the BMC which in turn becomes an implementable business plan.

By and large I have noticed that entrepreneurs are reluctant to do homework. They go for a mentor because they expect the mentor to do the homework for them. There is also a great reluctance to document anything. In our process of mentoring, we lay tremendous emphasis on not just the milestones but also the documentation. So at the end of each mentoring-call (which is recorded) I share not only the audio of the call but a document called 'Action Points' which the mentee is expected to complete before the next call. Typically, the action point will be around one of the nine building blocks.

Many claim that it is all there in their heads but they are not able to document it. My worry is, if they can't document it, how in the world will they ever communicate it to their stakeholders? Maybe in the future with a wearable device, customers, investors and teams can simply scan the entrepreneur's brain to read his thoughts but till then they have no option but to document it!

2. Waive all my problems away with your magic wand!

This is a serious and most unreasonable expectation. Usually this expectation is not from startups but mature enterprises. When their portfolio of problems becomes larger than their portfolio of customers, they see merit in having a mentor. An entrepreneur in his forties told me guilelessly that he came to me because he heard me saying in various media platforms that having a mentor is excellent risk-mitigation strategy. Except that in his case, he had already exposed his company to every possible risk with a series of bad decisions and when the investors had threatened to oust him, he came to me to clean up the mess.

3. Find me an investor

Most entrepreneurs approach us with the expectation that we will connect them to investors, even when the business idea is just a concept in their head and they are a long way off from becoming investment-worthy. But most of them think that their idea is brilliant and therefore not only customers but also investors will and should queue up at their doorstep!

4. Be my 'yes' man!

Some entrepreneurs opt for mentoring simply to confirm that their idea is brilliant. Such people are difficult to handle because they brook no criticism. I have had instances where an entrepreneur has told me either on the call or through an email later that he did not like the way I critiqued some of his ideas, because after all "I have ten years of work experience in an MNC". How do I tell him that his work experience means nothing if he hasn't learnt the basics of management?

The right attitude for mentorship

When you seek a mentor, you should be mentor-ready. What do I mean by this? It means you should have the right attitude. What constitutes the right attitude? One is the implicit trust that your mentor is in your corner. So if he tells you things that you don't want to hear, it is not that he wants to belittle you but because he has the interest of your company at heart. Since he is not involved in the day-to-day running of your company, he is able to distance himself enough to retain his objectivity. So he may see things that you miss because you are so immersed in the business. It is a very talk-listen engagement with the both of you doing both the things in equal measure.

I have also realized that many entrepreneurs are stubborn creatures. In my early days of mentoring, the stubbornness used to frustrate me. Over time, I have learned to work around it, gently nudging my mentees to change their attitude and approach without seeming to do so.

In the last ten years of mentoring, I have seen mentees with diverse approaches and attitudes. To understand their approach better, I put them in the following buckets:

❖ The Techies who know their domain inside-out, but little else. They are mostly engineers, under 30 years, working in a large IT organization as part of a technical team. I find them easy to mentor because they are clear on what they know and what they don't know. So they have an open attitude towards mentoring. I enjoy mentoring them because I get to learn tech-speak! The first time I heard a mentee mention Ruby on Rails (it is a web application framework, written in Ruby, which is a programming language), I had this vision of a glitzy Marilyn Monroe-like woman named Ruby holding on to her dress on a rail track!

❖ The Middle-agers who have had nearly two decades of work experience in large IT firms and have even worked overseas. They come with a fair amount of their own network. They seek a mentor because they know it is the one thing in the Silicon Valley that makes them seem more evolved. I love my mentoring calls with them because they bring a lot of breadth to the conversations, especially in the ideation phase. But when they get down to implementing, they frustrate the life out of me because they make decisions which belie their age and experience!

For example, they may hire people not because of their competency but because they had worked together in the previous company. Not just worked together, but they had bonded well, because they all had hated their boss!

Similarly, they may sign a service level agreement (SLA) with a customer with terms that are detrimental to their interest. Or, they may agree to divest their equity for a ludicrously low valuation. Or – and this is my pet peeve – they may be extremely sloppy in their documentation, especially those that have serious legal implications. Such mentees consume a lot of my bandwidth!

❖ The Passionistas, who are convinced that God sent them to planet earth so that they can do unlimited good. These are the good guys with the heart in the right place but the only problem is that they hate the color of money. They have lovely ideas but they are not only clueless on monetization but they have an active aversion to making money from their business. I love these guys because they want to change the world. However, they can't seem to wrap their do-gooding head around the fact that changing the world needs money and if they don't have a definite revenue-generating plan, their dreams will collapse. I have to be the mercenary mentor in this engagement!

❖ The Methodicals do everything by the book. They do all the homework, and make wise choices. They dot their i's and cross their t's. Very easy to mentor them, they understand and gravitate to the process of mentoring with alacrity; by and large they have a dream run. I love mentoring them

❖ The Vanishers talk big but they disappear after a couple of calls. They are a mixed bag of young and old people. They claim they have the prototype of their product ready. They may also claim that they already have one big customer in the bag. Money is no object. They need a mentor just to stitch it all together, they say.

After the second or the third call, they vamoose, and are never heard of again. My repeated mails will elicit either no response or a very terse 'working on action points, will revert when done'. Sometimes they bail out by saying, 'I have to go to the US on a company assignment for six months, will resume when I'm back'.

❖ The B-schoolers. They may be engineers, commerce or management undergrads, who have armed themselves with a management degree from high-end schools or unheard-of schools, from metro cities or Tier II towns, from convent schools or vernacular medium schools. It doesn't matter where they are from or what their backgrounds are. Pedigree doesn't make their behavior any different. They sincerely believe that by virtue of their MBA, they are now ready only for a CEO position.

So when they join large organizations, they are easily frustrated because no one else seems to think that they are CEO material and are expected to do all the grunge work like the others. And when they become entrepreneurs, they call themselves CEO from day one without having a clue about managing the business. I find mentoring them the hardest because they are simply not amenable to learning.

Summary

It doesn't matter which bucket the entrepreneur falls in. The fact is I love mentoring. At my age I think I can say, without sounding pompous, mentoring has made me more learned, quite like Saul Bellow's hero, and a better human being.

TAKEAWAYS

- Mentors are a must-have, not good-to-have, for every entrepreneur. Because having a mentor is excellent risk-mitigation strategy
- Mentors bring, not just knowledge, skill and attitude to the table, but also their network and that is priceless to an entrepreneur at all stages of his business
- Entrepreneurs need mentors with different skill-sets at different stages of the business.
- Mentoring is a two-way street. Both mentor and mentee need to have the right attitude
- It is a relationship as much based on empathy and trust as on knowledge

WHY ENTREPRENEURS SHOULD DO A COURSE IN ORGANIZATION BEHAVIOR

> " Just because you are CEO, don't think
> you have landed. You must continuously
> increase your learning, the way you think and
> the way you approach the organization "
>
> – Indra Nooyi, Chairperson &CEO of PepsiCo.

I OFTEN GET MAILS from youngsters, asking if an MBA is a must
for becoming an entrepreneur. Typically these mails are from
engineering graduates: some of them have just graduated and some
are in the process. There must be tremendous societal pressure on
them to enroll for an MBA. Some of them are already exploring
a business idea. As it happens with engineering students, they
may have technical knowledge but are all at sea when it comes to
building the business around their idea.

There is a course called New Venture Creation, somewhere in
the sixth term, offered in many engineering schools. The course is
actually supposed to teach them how to commercialize a business
idea. It includes all the things that one needs to do to get a concept
off his head into the marketplace.

The travesty is that in many engineering schools there is no designated or competent person to teach the course. I have seen that, in some schools, the head of the mechanical department teaches the course. In others, whichever teacher has a lighter teaching load that term is assigned to it. And even if they have a management professor, he is an academician who has never walked through the portals of a corporate office. How would he know about creating an organization around a business idea?

This is why engineering students who want to become entrepreneurs mail me the one question that is bothering them: Is an MBA necessary to become an entrepreneur?

Now, let's look at whether an MBA really prepares an engineering student to become an entrepreneur.

For over a decade now, I have been offering a purchase course in entrepreneurship in business schools across the world. I make it a point to offer this course only in their last semester so that all their basic management concepts are in place, before they sign up for entrepreneurship. One thing I have noticed is most business schools lay emphasis on finance, marketing, human resources, operations but they rarely give primacy to a subject called organization behavior or OB as it is popularly called.

All the business schools offer OB either in the first or second term and the teacher is usually someone who has a doctorate in management. As an academician, he will teach all the concepts theoretically. Even if he is a great teacher, he still fails to drive home the importance of OB concepts in a corporate environment. Add to this the fact that majority of the class have an engineering background with no knowledge of social sciences. So when OB is taught to them, theoretically, and not as an application framework, they are either indifferent to what is in it and its relevance to their corporate stints or they develop a certain amount of derision for this course as it all seems like such a lark.

At the end of the term, placements happen and they are launched on their corporate careers. Some of them, the smart ones, quickly learn on the fly to navigate the corporate labyrinth. Some of them get tossed about and chewed in the corporate centrifuge. Watching them, all at sea, my heart aches, knowing that their OB teacher did not do justice to the subject. To my mind, OB is the foundation on which management education is built.

Management is called the 'bastard science' because it does not have a single original concept. Everything is borrowed from other sciences, predominantly social sciences. OB is defined as a science that studies what people think, feel and do in organizations. In other words, it is the study of human behavior inside organizations.

The amazing gamut it covers are individual values that owners and employees bring to the workplace, their emotions and attitudes; how they motivate themselves and others; how they design the processes of decision making and how consensus and conflict resolution are a critical piece of this design. Also included is how behavior is not only influenced by perception but can be modified by learning; how high performance teams can be built without subjecting them to stratospheric stress levels.

It also covers the importance of cultivating effectively communicating teams that talk and listen in equal measure, the role and reach of power in defining the hierarchical dynamics within the office and the necessity of identifying relevant leadership. It answers questions such as why every employee should be trained in the art of negotiation and why one should accept that change is the only constant within any organization. All of this goes on to create what is called organization culture, which is nothing but the way people do things within an organization, the structures, systems and processes that foster this culture and determine its efficacy for the organization.

Is there anything in what I have highlighted above that is not relevant for a management student aspiring to become a manager in an organization or an entrepreneur wanting to start off on his own? The pity is that here is a course that can give you the best equipment to build your strengths from within and get you so ready for your corporate/entrepreneurial journey from the word go. Yet, it is given the short shrift by both teachers and students.

The irony is that the courses that are given importance to, in the business school, such as marketing, human resources, operations, finance and strategy, are themselves built on the foundation laid by OB. Marketing is all about connecting with your customers on an emotional level and hence managing their perceptions. Finance teaches fiscal discipline and good corporate governance practices which are in the realm of sound business principles. Human resources is all about fostering an organization's culture that encourages its employees to cultivate a scientific temper that helps them innovate and learn to become high performers. Strategic vision deals with the exciting subject of reifying the organization's values so that it can assume a leadership position in the marketplace.

Why then, this step-motherly treatment to OB? Is it ignorance, carelessness or is it simply that we are stuck in a time warp? Are we saying, this is how we have been teaching management since the British introduced it in the military in India towards the end of the 19th century and even when times and climes have changed, we will continue to do so?

I think the time has come to design management education around the core precepts of OB! Why only management education, in fact I would go as far as to say that every employee in your organization should go through a crash course in OB during his induction phase. So my response to all those who mail me, asking if an MBA is necessary to become an entrepreneur is, if you are particular about an MBA degree, choose a business school that offers you good grounding in OB. But if you want to get off on your entrepreneurial journey right away, give yourself three months to do a DIY course in OB. There is more than enough material out there on the internet, it may not fetch you a certificate but it will prepare you for your entrepreneurial journey and enrich your life.

It requires a good understanding of the psychology of the customer in order to effect behavioral changes. That understanding comes in an encapsulated form from the study of OB. So even if there is no course in OB, it is an easy and imagination-grabbing DIY learning. Engage in it for your own benefit. Not just when you decide to become an entrepreneur but even as an employee in your organization.

Summary

Gone are the days when an entrepreneur was expected to give the customer what the customer wants. In today's context, an entrepreneur is expected to give the customer what the customer does not even know he wants! In other words, he is expected to be the architect of change in user behavior. He is expected to create products that hook the customer into using them which in turn become so habit-forming that they become integral to his life and the customer is left wondering: how did I manage before?

TAKEAWAYS

- Do an MBA before becoming an entrepreneur in a business school that gives primacy to OB
- If you don't want to do an MBA, give yourself three months to learn the principles of OB on your own. It will help you manage the ups and downs of your entrepreneurial journey with knowledge and equanimity

SUTRA VI

HOW DO YOU CREATE ADDICTION FOR YOUR PRODUCTS?

> 66 **Did anyone ever tell you that changing the world looks good on you?** 99
>
> – A post on unreasonable.org

I MUST CONFESS, right at the beginning of writing this chapter, that I was hugely influenced by two seminal books. One is Nir Eyal's *Hooked*. The other is *Addiction by Design* by Natasha Schull. Let me discuss them, one by one.

I first came across Nir Eyal, may be three or four years ago, when I stumbled on his blog called *nirandfar*. It was the word-play on his name that caught my attention and very casually I started to read. I found his style engaging. What captivated me was that he wrote about "the intersection of psychology, technology and business, (called) 'behavioral design'. The topic encompasses user experience, behavioral economics and a dash of neuroscience" (Source: nirandfar.com).

Nir is an MBA from the Stanford Graduate School of Business. He speaks passionately and extensively on how to 'hook' your customers by creating habit-forming products. He says, "*I embarked upon a journey to learn how products change our actions, and at times, create compulsions. How did these companies engineer user behavior? What were the moral implications of building potentially addictive products? Most important, could the same forces that made these experiences so compelling also be used to build products to improve people's lives?"* 'Potentially addictive products' does not refer to any kind of substance abuse products at all. It refers only to good products and there is no moral dilemma here. The product may become so addictive that it may cause an irritation to others around you but it does not endanger life; on the contrary, it may affect your life positively.

Let me give you an example. Empirical studies have shown that most people who use smart phones look at their phones the moment they wake up. It has been established that this indeed is addictive behavior and this addiction may cause huge irritation in their respective spouses. At the same time, it helps them stay connected with their world and in some cases on top of situations. But sometimes people may take this addiction a tad too far. Nir talks about a study which showed that people preferred their phone-time to sex!

Addiction by Design is about machine gambling in Las Vegas. Schull, a cultural anthropologist and associate professor at MIT, started her research on 'addiction at the slot machines' as a graduate student and continued with it for her post-doctoral research too.

Nir recommended the book, *Addiction by Design*, written by Natasha Dow Schüll, in one of his lectures, if I remember correctly. It is an un-put-down-able book. Every page that I turned gave me heebie-jeebies. It was frightening in a very Hitchcockian way, to say the least.

Whilst Nir obsessed about how to create a product design that will become a habit with its customers, Schull researched into why a simple habit can become crushingly addictive. Up until that point in time, both physicians and psychologists believed that addiction as it is generally understood (dictionary definition is *'the state of being enslaved to a product….to such an extent that its cessation causes severe trauma'*) was a genetic phenomenon, therefore, only certain people with those genes had the proclivity to addiction, whether it was substance abuse or gambling. There was also an economic class associated with addiction; simplistically, very poor or very rich people had the proclivity towards addiction.

Schull's study proved conclusively that addiction had no correlation to class, genes, gender or age. People who were addicted to machine gambling came from all walks of life. So she surmised that perhaps people become addicted to gambling because they want to win. Mollie, one of her research 'addictees', beautifully busted this myth when she said: we all know nothing lasts; not winning, not losing. We know if we are winning, there will come a time when we will start to lose. And vice versa. So it is not winning or the prospect of a big win that makes us gamble away.

Why then do you play Mollie, if not for winning? asked, Schull. The answer was spine-chilling. Mollie said, "(to) keep playing – to stay in that machine zone where nothing else matters".

I said Mollie's answer was spine-chilling because this obsession with 'staying in that machine zone' resulted in some seriously bizarre behavior. Such as, people coming to the gaming zones on Friday morning, wearing diapers so that they did not have to vacate their seat in front of the slot machine till Monday morning, even to go to the loo!

The question I am trying to address in this chapter is, how can you, as an entrepreneur, build habit-forming products; products that change the behavior of their users in such a way that the users can't remember a time when there were no such products? Is there a blueprint that can be adopted by every entrepreneur?

I am referencing gaming addiction to drive home the point that human behavior can be changed over time and based on situational stimuli. The behavior is evidenced and modified even without any trigger at all, thanks to the habit forming product that changed the behavior in the first place. But in doing so, I am going one step ahead of both Nir and Schull. I am saying that just forming a new habit is not good enough. It is imperative that your product becomes an integral part of your customer's life. Simply because it makes them manage their lives better. Remember, that is why you became an entrepreneur in the first place – to improve people's lives by changing their behavior.

Inducing habit-forming behavior is a survival imperative for entrepreneurs. But this alone is not enough. We all know we are in the habit of checking our smart phones, not just first thing when we wake up but also the last thing before going to bed. Smart phones have been responsible for changing our behavior from using phones simply for calls in the good old days, to managing our entire lives on the phone, today. But within this realm of user behavior, what can smart phone brands do to become addictive? What makes an Apple lover an Apple lover? What makes Apple addictive? In other words, how could products be designed in such a way that by virtue of their very design they create addiction in the user and not because of external inducements?

> In other words, as Nir, said, while explaining his Hook Model, 'through consecutive Hook cycles, successful products reach their ultimate goal of unprompted user engagement, bringing users back repeatedly, without depending on costly advertising or aggressive messaging'.

So what is this Hook Model and how have some of the entrepreneurs used it to their advantage?

Source: *Hooked by NirEyal*

Trigger

Trigger refers to the stimulus that makes the user pause and take note that there is something 'else' on the horizon; something different from what he was used to. Let me share an example with you. For years, I have used Colgate toothpaste. Only one odd time, I bought Close-Up because either my local grocer did not have Colgate or by mistake I have picked it off the shelf in super market.

One night, I stayed at a friend's place in Delhi. Since it was an unplanned stay, I had to borrow her toothpaste. She had a brand called *Patanjali* in her bathroom. I did not like the color of the toothpaste (it was dark brown) but I liked the packaging. I am not a great fan of ayurvedic products, but I had read, just the previous day in *The Economic Times*, that Baba Ramdev's company had a turnover of Rs 2600 crores and was expected to touch Rs 5000 crores in FY 2015-16. So I decided to try it, not that I had any other option. Much to my surprise, I liked the taste of the toothpaste. Now this was an external trigger.

It was a happy coincidence that in less than 24 hours, I had been pleasantly surprised by a newspaper report on Patanjali's phenomenal success and had been presented with the opportunity of using the product, without choice. I forgot all about it over the next two days.

On day three, I was on my way back to Goa where I decided to stop at another friend's place for lunch before heading to airport. After lunch, I went to her bathroom to brush my teeth. And what do you know; she had Patanjali toothpaste in a mug! She also had Colgate. I remembered that when I used Patanjali at my friend's place previously, not only had I liked the taste, I had also loved the fresh feeling it left me with, even at the end of the day. Little wonder that I picked Patanjali over Colgate.

This was reinforced by the fact that after my second trial, I was as happy with the fresh feeling it caused in my mouth (and therefore in me) as the first time. This was the internal trigger.

Action

The internal trigger was so strong that when I reached Goa, the first thing I did was to Google the nearest Patanjali outlet. It wasn't close by; it was a pokey little shop run by a dour lady. There hardly seemed to be any customers and there was nothing in the shop to excite me into buying the toothpaste. But I did buy. It has been six months since I switched to Patanjali toothpaste and I haven't been tempted to buy Colgate at all, notwithstanding that it is so much easier to lay my hands on.

Variable Reward

It didn't stop with just the toothpaste. For years I have only bought Sunsilk shampoo (I might have bought Tresemme once in a way!). Suddenly, I decided to try Patanjali Natural shampoo. Needless to say I loved it. I bought all the three variants that the shop had; Natural, Shikakai and Reetha. And I loved them all. Next, I bought Patanjali bathing soap. Not just that but all its variants (Haldi, Chandan and MultaniMitthi). I loved those as well.

Then I did something so uncharacteristic that I knew I was 'hooked'. I went to the shop and asked if they had massage oil! They did and I romped home with it. Again, for years I have used either Body Shop or Bajaj Almond Oil and I had been extremely happy with both. I had never ever consciously thought of changing the brand or my behavior. But change I did.

I can only explain this abrupt change in behavior to the 'craving' I felt for Patanjali products!

Investment

I knew I was in for a repeat 'hook' cycle, not just once but several times. I not only told my friends about Patanjali but coaxed them into buying and dismissed their fears (one of my friends said she was afraid to use Patanjali because she had read somewhere that they use cow urine – '*gow mutra*' – in their products. I vehemently denied it). I discussed the brand in my entrepreneurship classes as an emerging global Indian brand, and now I'm writing about it! How much more invested in the product can I be? How much more 'hooked' can I be?

What was there in Patanjali's product design that hooked me, hook, line and sinker? How did Patanjali convert a non-customer (one who never used not just Patanjali but any Ayurvedic products) like me to not only use the product but become a Patanjali addict? As Steve Jobs said, product design is not about how it looks but what it does. Obviously Patanjali's product design 'did' a lot of good things to me. I must clarify something at this point here. When I say 'did', I don't mean that the toothpaste gave me the whitest smile or the shampoo made my hair long and lustrous or the soap gave me clear skin or the massage oil made my skin glow! Not at all. In fact, I think the beauty of the product design is in what it doesn't do!

Let me explain. The toothpaste kept my mouth so fresh for so long that I didn't need to brush on the hour. I loved the taste of the herbs and spices but they were important insofar as it reduced the incidence of my brushing. The soap didn't dry up my skin even in the winter months. I didn't feel that dryness around my mouth and under my eyes which I felt with other soaps after a hot shower. The shampoo didn't roughen up my hair. Sometimes when I gel and spike my hair, it changes the texture of my hair after a wash. With Patanjali, I could remove the gel without much ado and my hair went back to its pre-gel texture. My masseuse said she liked giving me massage with Patanjali oil because it did not make the contact on my skin dry, granular and jerky.

Even the packaging of all these products is easy on the eye (white-based), classy and very unlike the other products in its category (ayurvedic). The toothpaste flows through easily when squeezed but not so freely that it messes around the cap. The lid of the shampoo shuts firmly (a big plus when you're traveling). The oil is neither too thick nor too thin, just the right consistency and has a subtle aroma, not the cloying fragrance of other ayurvedic oils. All in all, Patanjali is a lovely FMCG brand with excellent product design.

So obviously with each of the products, a lot of research has gone into understanding the pain points and then creating a compelling customer experience from that understanding. This is a huge plus for its product design. It is not as if there are no downsides to the product design. Having created an excellent product, I wish Baba Ramdev's marketing team got inventive in their choice of channels. Right now, the products are available only in their own outlets and in some metros with local chemists and that is the most painful part about engaging with this brand. In Goa where I live, it is available only in brand-owned outlets. Even in Bangalore, I haven't found chemists stocking it in the Jayanagar area where I live in the city. That is the product design flaw as on date, the one they need to focus on to improve their product reach.

Recently, I read that the group has tied up with Big Bazaar. I understand that they have tied up with Gurgaon-based hyper-local delivery startup called Pluss as well to sell their entire range of products through Pluss's mobile app. I say, more the merrier!

Hopefully they will soon be available in every mom-and-pop store, in every super market and in every retail chain. Simply everywhere. This will certainly improve their product design and embellish customer experience.

Summary

A product is said to be behavior-changing if it entices, hooks and addicts the customer by its sheer design superiority and not by virtue of spending beaucoup bucks on aggressive messaging. As an entrepreneur, it is your *dharma* to create such products. As Nir says in his book *Hooked,* 'building habit-forming products is indeed a super power. If used irresponsibly, bad habits can quickly degenerate into mindless zombie-like addictions'. But we are not talking about bad products or addiction to bad products. We are talking about re-engineering old, entrenched habits with new, disruptive products that make your life better and make the world a nicer place.

Ray Kurzwell, the genius inventor, predictor of technological singularity and head of Google's engineering lab predicts that 'in our lifetime, we will experience 20,000 years of progress, based on how fast technology advances and affects human life. Experts say that in the next 20 years alone, we will experience more changes than in all of human history'. Some of the technologies that one can expect by 2030 include anti-aging treatments, pillows to share dreams, artificial intelligence personal assistants, digital contact lens, implanted mobile devices, exoskeletons, 3D printed liver transplants, and augmented reality (Source: *The Economic Times Magazine*, dated January 31-February 6, 2016). You don't need an expert to tell you how these products will change human behavior and have the potential to become addictive, over time.

TAKEAWAYS

- Design is what design does. Entrepreneurs should focus on products that are designed around making customer's life better. They will then automatically create addictive products

- There is no moral dilemma here as we are talking about good products that improve human lives and create good habits

- The product design should keep in mind the four stages of the Hook Loop – trigger, action, variable reward and investment

- Entrepreneurship is not just a journey of building products to cater to a need or bridge a gap in the marketplace. It is a pledge of creating meaningful products to your customers, thereby embellishing their user experience

HOW DO YOU TRANSITION FROM AN ENTREPRENEUR TO A BUSINESS LEADER?

> **Two things define you. Your patience, when you have nothing, and your attitude, when you have everything**
>
> – Unknown

THE ENTREPRENEURIAL JOURNEY IS a very strange thing. When you start building a product, your biggest strength is your domain. You know a lot about it but you know very little about building a business around it. Let us say, knowing that you don't know, you find yourself a mentor and do everything to become market-ready.

In the process, you wear several hats and juggle all the roles. You are the owner, the CEO, the marketer, the bookkeeper and the pantry boy – all rolled into one. It is not easy but you learn to do it because you know it is not enough to build a great product. You also need to build a great business around it. But at heart, you are a product specialist and you keep returning to it at every available opportunity.

Then, one day, your company becomes big. You have multiple offices, large teams, branded products and huge mindshare of your customers. Investors find your business attractive and they come on board to fuel your growth. At this stage you suddenly realize that it is not enough if you are an entrepreneur. You need to become a business leader. If you don't make this transition, two things will happen. One, you may yourself become the showstopper for your business, catapulting into the big league. Two, realizing that you may become the showstopper, your investors may show you the door.

As an entrepreneur, this is your moment of truth, the one no one talks about. It is the elephant in the room. At what point in your entrepreneurial journey should you stop being an entrepreneur and emerge as a strategic thinker? Is it when your product hits the market? Is it when your team size grows from one to fifty? Is it when your story is written about in *The Economic Times*? Or is it when you bring an investor on board?

I don't think there is a formulaic answer to this question. Starting your journey as an entrepreneur is your egoistic trip. You are trying to pursue your dream, rest of the world be damned. It is an obsessively inward-looking journey. As you build the product and go to market, the business necessitates that you bring other stakeholders on board – teams, customers, partners, and investors. As you on-board each one of them, you lose a bit of egocentricity and gain out-worldliness. Now it is no longer just your dream; you have to balance it with the dream of all your stakeholders without losing the original plot. How well you balance this not only determines how good a leader you are but essentially this is the beginning of your transition.

> Zuckerberg launched Facebook along with four other classmates from his dorm at Harvard and by the time he turned 23, he was a billionaire; thanks to Facebook's success.

I also suspect that leadership develops at different stages in different people. It may be thrust on a twenty-two-year old campus entrepreneur by the exigencies of his business, sooner than later. Mark Eliott Zuckerberg is a case in point.

If you were to take a peek into Zuckerberg's early life, there is nothing to indicate that he had this leadership potential. In high school, he excelled at classics, his classmates remember him reciting lines from epics such as Homer's *The Iliad*. He excelled in Mathematics, Physics and Astronomy and somewhere along the way he became fascinated by computers and developed an interest in writing algorithms and developing software.

Nothing in this profile indicates that Zuckerberg had it in him to become a billionaire at 23. In fact, when he launched Facebook, he had no intention of making money from it. He kept repeating that 'we are trying to help people connect and communicate more efficiently' adding that 'by giving people the power to share we're making the world more transparent'. When did he realize the full business potential of what he had unleashed?

I have heard a variety of answers from successful entrepreneurs on when they transitioned. Some said that they became leaders when they realized that they had multiple stakeholders who had high expectations of them. Others said that they were forced to become leaders when they failed. Many have told me that they were fortunate in having a good mentor who groomed them into becoming responsible leaders.

My take is a little different. I think that in the early days of your entrepreneurial journey, you make decisions largely based on a combination of your own nature, your exposure and the resources on hand. Let me illustrate this. In the pre-market days, if one of your developers quits, because you wouldn't entertain his request for a raise, your typical reaction would be as follows:

If you are a 22-something – generally popular in college, go-getter kind of guy and you are developing your product from money scrounged from what your dad sends you for studies and hostel – your first reaction is to take him out for a smoke and talk him out of it. You will show him the big picture; how disruptive your product is and how one day, all of you will become millionaires. If he still doesn't bite, you will pat him on his back and say, no problem dude, I understand, let me know if you know someone as good as you. And you part on good terms.

If you are a 30-something with about six years of work experience and developing your product with the money you saved from your salary and overseas travel, your typical reaction will be to impress upon him that he cannot leave till he has completed the task at hand because 'you cannot let me down at this stage'. You may even buy time by admonishing him to complete the work. You may even dangle a carrot by saying that if he does stay, you will give him a raise.

If you are a 40-something and have returned to India after working on-site for an IT MNC and you have not only saved enough money to develop the product but you have stitched up an alliance with people in your network for funding, your standard reaction will be: no way Jose, please check your appointment letter. It says very clearly that you have to give us three months' notice during which you have to complete your tasks, groom the new incumbent and properly hand over to him before leaving. And by the way, we say very clearly in the appointment letter that performance review is only once a year and increment is linked to that.

In the first scenario, your leadership style is to take bad news in your stride because you don't know enough to allow it to faze you. In the second, because you are probably older than your developer, your leadership style is to invoke emotion and loyalty. In the third, your leadership style is distinctly contractual.

The point I'm making is that in your early days of entrepreneurship, you do demonstrate some leadership traits but they are largely those that come naturally to you. As you build the company, you learn new traits.

There is a story that Zuckerberg hated communicating with his employees and in the early days, he would simply disappear, leaving his team bewildered and lost. He was simply uncommunicative. One day, one of his colleagues told him that this leadership style wouldn't win him brownie points and that as a CEO he had to learn to seem more forthcoming. He listened and his company benefited from the vibrancy of his team. The truth is that there is no one single point in your journey that can be ear-marked to say that is the point when you transition from an entrepreneur to a leader. I think the correct way of saying is you are a leader when you behave like one.

So what are the traits of a leader? In management books, leadership is over-glorified and leaders are made to look like gods. It took someone like Steve Jobs to demonstrate that you may have all the frailty as a human being but when it came to building a company, you could be a leader par excellence. To my mind, there is one umbrella requirement for being branded an excellent leader. He should have, in equal measure, what I call *Garuda Drishti* (eagle view) and *Sarpa Drishti* (snake view).

Garuda Dhrishti and Sarpa Drishti

In your grandparents' puja room, you must have seen Lord Vishnu's photographs. In some, he is depicted as riding on the back of the eagle. In others, he is seen lying supine on a snake, resting against its raised hood. What is the significance of both these scenarios?

Go back to your basics. In the scheme of things, the Universe is supposed to be governed by the trinity of Brahma, Vishnu and Shiva. Each has a specific role. Brahma is the creator, Vishnu is the perpetuator and Shiva is the destroyer. On the face of it, all three seem to have roles that are contrarian to each other.

How can Brahma create something new when Vishnu is hell-bent on preserving the old that Shiva is equally determined to destroy? The answer is simple and perhaps explains why the universe continues to exist in an orderly manner.

Brahma creates new things. Vishnu preserves what is best from the old and integrates it into the new, seamlessly. Shiva destroys what is harmful from the old so that a good new order is breathed into the universe.

Now to perform his role of a preserver, what skill-set does Vishnu require? Primarily, he needs two things. One, he needs the overview of the whole universe the big picture —what is called in management as the 30,000-feet view. Because it is here that he gets a bird's eye view of all that's happening. Hence, Vishnu is depicted as riding on the back of the eagle. This is called Garuda Drishti (Sanskrit phrase meaning, eagle view).

But is this enough to be a leader? Obviously not. He also needs a detailed view of important things so that he can make a judgment call as to what should stay and what should go. In other words, he needs an eye for detail of the ground-level realities. Hence he is shown lying on the serpent. This is called Sarpa Drishti (Sanskrit phrase meaning, snake view).

I think people will see the emergence of a leader when they see a combination of Garuda Drishti and Sarpa Drishti in you. In the product development phase, you are obsessed only about your product to the exclusion of everything else. So much so, you do not even bother about who would buy this product. But as you built the business, your focus expands to areas beyond the product such as your customer, team, resources, partners, competitors, media and government regulations as well. It is at this stage that you begin to acquire Garuda Drishti. But this does not mean that you lose sight of what is happening at the ground level. You cannot say, I was so busy looking at the big picture that I did not realize that someone in my team was selling secrets to our competitors! You need to have Sarpa Drishti in equal measure.

This is an exciting transition for you, where you move from 'dhyana' (Sanskrit word for focus) to 'darshana' (Sanskrit word for perspective). What an enviable journey!

Let us look at the use case of Zomato to understand this balance in its co-founders.

Deepinder Goyal and Pankaj Chaddha started Zomato in 2008 as a restaurant-listing platform. At that time, both were employees of Bain Consulting. How did they get the idea for Zomato? At lunchtime every day, they saw their colleagues poring over physical copies of several cafeteria menus. The two decided to save them some time, so they put up scanned copies of the menus on the company intranet.

It soon caught everyone's imagination and the two of them quit their jobs and started Foodiebay, which was a restaurant listing site in NCR (National Capital Region which includes Delhi, Faridabad, Gurgaon and Noida). By 2011, they raised capital from Info Edge, changed the name to Zomato and entered other metros of India.

Between mid-2014 and 2015, they made nine acquisitions in different countries, including a very popular brand called Urbanspoon in the United States. It is the second biggest company in the world in this space; Yelp being the biggest with its presence in 32 countries. By early 2016, they listed 1.4 million restaurants across 10,000 cities in 22 countries and planned to expand their footprint to eight more geographies by March 2016.

In late 2015, they also announced that they would not only list restaurants but would also get into the food delivery space, competing with the likes of Foodpanda and TinyOwl (both companies have begun to see a downturn with serious issues of their own).

How did Zomato demonstrate this kind of market leadership in less than 7 years? I think the answer lies in the quality of leadership at the helm. One story of the founders particularly impressed me. A few months before they acquired Urbanspoon, they had changed the company logo. As usual, some liked it, others didn't. There was a tremendous feeding frenzy on the social media. Then they announced the acquisition of Urbanspoon, which not only gave them the enviable footprint in North America and Canada, but also added a heavy weight brand to their portfolio. Very soon the founders realized that Urbanspoon enjoyed a huge mindshare amongst its customers in the US and Canada and its simple logo had as much recall as the M of McDonald. So the big question was: since Zomato had acquired it, should Urbanspoon also use the Zomato logo or should it continue to use its old one in the US?

The company could very well have decided to keep the Zomato logo for the Indian market and the Urbanspoon logo for the North American and Canadian markets, concurrently. But they took a call to do away with the Zomato logo (which was barely a few months old) and migrated the Urbanspoon logo across the board. Logic? Urbanspoon had more brand power!

To my mind, this is an excellent illustration of the balance between Garuda Drishti and Sarpa Drishti in a leader. So what does possessing this balance mean? How is it demonstrable?

There are a number of ways in which this can be demonstrated. I will list five of them here which I think are of paramount importance. They are:

- ❖ Market disruption
- ❖ Customer engagement
- ❖ Consistency
- ❖ Personal growth
- ❖ Conquest of fear

Let us look at what each one of these entails.

Market disruption

This is about seducing your customer. There was a time when marketers lived by the mantra of 'give the customer what he wants'. There came a time when that wasn't enough and they realized that in order to survive in a highly competitive market, they had to 'give the customer more than what he wants'. In the last five years or so, thanks to the new age internet companies which are finding more and more innovative ways of gaining wallet-share of their customers, the mantra has changed to a rather radical 'give the customer what he never even knew he wanted'!

American shoe company Converse, which was started in 1908 and acquired by Nike in 2003, is an excellent example of this. Marquis Mill Converse started by making galoshes, or rubber-soled boots that were good for winter wear. He then added canvas shoes which became hugely popular with tennis and basketball players. So at some point the company became popular as a 'sneaker' shoes manufacturer. This gave him an idea. He got tennis and basketball players to endorse his brand. They did so happily. He then enticed customers by offering to customize their shoes by printing pictures of their favorite sportsmen. The customers went crazy.

All the while he kept the price point low. Given the high profile sportsmen who endorsed his brand, he could very easily have made it into a premium product. But his logic was that his product should be affordable to as many people as possible because more the people buy it, the more they will talk about it.

Up until then, sports shoes were hugely expensive and only those who had serious purchasing power could afford it. Now with price points being low, not only more people could buy it, many of them could even aspire to become sportsmen like their favorite icons! They were simply blown away!

Customer engagement

This is about being on the same page as your customer. I heard this story some time ago and I am sharing it here as it illustrates my point. Rekha had a toothache and she went to a dentist. As she sat in the reception of the clinic, she noticed that there was a certificate of the dentist with his picture, hanging on the wall. The name of the dentist was Kunal. Rekha smiled for a minute. She thought to herself: when I was in eighth standard, I had a classmate called Kunal on whom I had a huge crush. He was so cute! She then looked at the picture and decided this fat, balding man could not possibly be the same Kunal. He looked much older than her, so he couldn't be her classmate! After some time, she was ushered into the dentist's chair and she noticed the dentist was not only fat and bald but had terrible skin too. She decided that he was no way 'her Kunal'!

Whilst the doctor was getting ready, she made small talk with him. She asked him perfunctory questions:

Are you from Mumbai?

Yes.

Where did you study?

Xavier's.

Then her eyes lit up. *Arre*, she said, I'm also from Xavier's. Which year did you do your 10th standard?

1983.

Oh my god, she said, I was there at the same time.

This time he looked at her and asked, oh, really, what subject did you teach us?

Horrible man, right? But imagine for a moment that Rekha is the entrepreneur and the dentist is the customer. Imagine if they were both so not on the same page!

I remember sitting through a business plan pitch from a mature entrepreneur (mature, both in age and experience) a couple of months ago. His retail outlet was called Farm Fresh and they sold fresh vegetables and fruits. His family owned large tracts of land where they grew vegetables and fruits. So the outlet was a logical forward integration for him. So far, so good.

When he started to discuss expansion plan, he veered off track. He said they have plans to add groceries, shampoos, hygiene products and soaps and the like. I was horrified. How were they Farm Fresh, I asked. He blubbered saying customers want a single window for everything.

From a good value proposition where he promised and delivered fresh vegetables and fruits (farm to fork), he was planning to mutilate the brand by becoming yet another super-market! Can you imagine the disconnect customers would feel, walking into a Farm Fresh outlet and seeing Cuticura talcum powder?

Be consistent

This is about being logical and cohesive in your internal and external communication, between what you say and what you do, in not just YOU walking the talk, but everyone in your team as well. I think this is perhaps the hardest leadership trait to demonstrate. Somehow in our Indian culture, we are taught to be all things to all people, even if one contradicts the other. So when we become entrepreneurs, we say, everyone is my customer! The inconsistency and incongruity of this is lost on us.

The best example for consistency is South West Airlines. There is a story about its legendary founder Herb Kelleher that illustrates this. One morning, one of his flight crew came to Herb's office with a suggestion. She said, everyday, on our first Boston-Washington flight at 6.30 am, we mostly have business travelers heading towards their meetings straightaway. So there is hardly any opportunity for them to have breakfast, either before boarding the plane or after disembarking. Why don't we offer them a *petit dejuner* (small breakfast)? It could be a sandwich or coffee with a cookie.

Herb heard her out patiently. Excellent Marianne, he said. I think it's a very thoughtful idea on your part. Who will pay for it, he asked?

Why, we will, of course, she said.

We are a no-frills, low-cost airline, Marianne, as you know. So our margins are already squeezed. Do you think we will be able to absorb this additional cost?

Right, she said, so we will charge the customer for breakfast.

In which case, Marianne, said Herb, the cost of flying will go up for the customer. How will we still be a low-cost airline?

Consistency is a very important ingredient of excellent leadership.

Personal growth

This is about investing in your own self. Entrepreneurs take a lot of pride that notwithstanding their meager resources, they invest in training their teams by nominating them for workshops, seminars and conferences of different themes. Great, but how about up-skilling yourself?

Somehow, there seems to be a feeling in the entrepreneur that if he nominates himself for, let's say, an app-building workshop, he's admitting to a certain vulnerability, In India, the moment we lead teams, we are expected to be a know-all, irrespective of age and experience. We invest in up-skilling our teams but never ourselves. So much so, there comes a point in time when our teams overtake us, leaving us pretty much at the same place where we started off. That obviously is not a healthy situation.

The biggest downfall of not investing in ourselves is that we lose the ability to interpret the macro picture or what in management is called connecting the dots. Let me illustrate this.

> A small team of 11 people, headed by an animator called John Lassiter made a remarkably groundbreaking movie called Toy Story in 1995. It was the first of its kind in digital animation. The name of the company was Pixar.

The success of Toy Story caused huge concern in one company and that was Disney. Disney has been a pioneer in animation and has been in business since 1923. It has a huge treasure chest of animation properties, yet one movie by an upstart called Pixar caused some serious anguish to Disney's management.

Bob Iger who was the president of Disney at that time said that it was not Disney's leadership style to wait for something to become a problem tomorrow. They preferred to take the situation head on, today, before it became a problem!

So what did Disney do? It bought out Pixar!

This kind of ability, to foresee a potential problem in the future and the vision to fix it today before it becomes a problem tomorrow, either comes with DNA or it has to be acquired by investing in oneself.

Conquest of fear

This is not about absence of fear or being absolutely fearless. This is about acknowledging that being afraid is natural and figuring out ways of overcoming it.

Some years ago, I had the opportunity of interviewing Nelson Mandela for a television channel. I was in awe of him and a couple of times, during the course of the interview, I said, you must be such a courageous man, sir, to have survived Robben Island. He dismissed it the first couple of times. When I repeated it the third time, he said, "Nandini, you don't get it. Every minute of my stay in Robben Island, I was petrified. But I couldn't obviously show it to my people who were looking up to me to get out and lead them. So my dear, he said, courage is not absence of fear. Courage is conquest of fear."

As an entrepreneur, every moment of your journey is as much fraught with uncertainty as excitement. Uncertainty results in fear (it could also be the other way).

When you hire people, you are afraid that you may not have it in you to lead them. When you build your products, you are not sure whether you will be able to convince your customers to buy them. As you start spending, you begin to worry whether the resources you have on hand will last you till you are able to raise money. And at the back of it all is the fear if you are entrepreneur material at all; whether you made a huge mistake sitting out of placements or kicking your well-paying job. The biggest fear of course is the fear of failure and the social stigma attached to it. How do you overcome all of this and forge ahead?

There are no shortcuts or formulaic solutions to this. I think the best way to address each one of the fear-inducing situations is by finding yourself a mentor who will not only help you overcome your fear but not let it cloud your judgment.

Summary

One of the done-to-death debates is whether leaders are born or can they be made. I think some are born and many others can be made. I refuse to accept that something as important as leadership, entrepreneurship, etc. can be left to the caprice of a DNA! Every entrepreneur has to dig out the leader from inside him and there is no such thing as the right time for it.

In my reckoning, the moment an entrepreneur starts building a business as an entity separate from his own persona, his leadership meter starts ticking.

TAKEAWAYS

- The transition from an entrepreneur to a business leader is a coming-of-age phenomenon for the entrepreneur
- There is no such thing as a right time for it. It is when the business exigencies demand it
- Being a leader means developing and balancing between Garuda Drishti and Sarpa Drishti
- The five elements of this drishti are market disruption, customer engagement, consistency, personal growth, and conquest of fear

SUTRA VIII

BUILDING A HIGH
PERFORMANCE CULTURE

> " " Set your course by the stars, not by the
> lights of every passing ship " "
>
> – Omar Bradley, US Army General

IN THE EARLY DAYS of your business, you are neither worried about building an organization nor fostering a culture. Your focus is only on developing your product and getting it out into marketplace, before somebody else does. I am making this statement based on my own experience as an entrepreneur and mentor.

Just the way I asked in the chapter on leadership, when do you become a leader, I'm asking again here. When do you begin to build the culture of your organization? Is it something that has to be carefully crafted or is it something that happens on its own? And who decides what kind of culture the organization should have?

Culture is what makes us human. However, this is being disputed by some recent studies which show that elephants and primates also have some kind of culture. For example, an elephant will never die in full public view: it gets a premonition of its death well in advance and seeks out a lonely cave to breathe its last. Similarly,

> Culture is a term borrowed by Management Science from Social Anthropology. It simply means shared set of values and beliefs among the members that guides their behavior. It could be in a family, in a temple, in a college or in an organization. The best way to remember culture is by the pithy phrase: the way we do things around here.

among baboons and chimpanzees, if one of their members dies, they will bury the dead and grieve loudly over the grave by screaming, dancing and chest beating. So if culture is iterative behavior, then it is not the exclusive preserve of the human race, but the jury is still out on whether iterative behavior has to be 'learned' to be called culture (in the elephants and the primates, it is 'instinctive' behavior).

Let's go with the simple definition of organization culture; it is the way people do things within the organization. What things, you may ask. Things like how we treat customers; how we groom employees; how we induct new hires; how we spend money; how we conduct ourselves in public spaces; how we lay out our offices; how we respond in crises. All of which is learned behavior.

But if all this is behavior, how is it culture? These are all behavioral manifestations of the values we hold that guide our thinking to dictate how we behave. So culture is not just the way we do things around here but it is the thought process of the values that we hold dear and beliefs that we cherish that make us do things the way we do. Let me explain this with the brilliant use case of Whole Foods (Source for the use case: Gary Hamel's book: *The Future of Management*).

> Whole Foods is an American supermarket chain that specializes in organic food. It was started in 1980 and by September 2015, it had 91000 employees, 431 outlets in US, Canada and UK. It became a Fortune 500 company in 2005.

Don't get misled by the term 'supermarket'. It is not your typical granny store. The supermarket offers you eye popping, mouth-watering, guilt-free gastronomy of organic and natural products at a premium. In fact, uncharitable people even call it "whole paycheck"!

John Mackey, the founder of Whole Foods, is a very colorful and evolved man. He keenly observed the US supermarket culture prevalent at that time around him and what struck him most was that:

❖ All of them loaded up factory food on their shelves

❖ Offered unviable discounts to drive demand

❖ Put pressure on suppliers to spend large amounts of money on advertising on national television to stoke demand

❖ Acquired mom-and-pop stores and smaller chains at peanut valuation by running down their business

This resulted naturally in anorexic margins, steadily plunging market shares, and humongous discontent among teams. So Mackey decided that his supermarket chain would be very different. He embraced a contrarian management model that promoted 'democracy with discipline', 'trust with accountability' and 'community with fierce internal competition'.

As you can see, he focused as much on his organization culture as on his product.

How did he implement this doctrine?

The starting point was to ask the basic question: who knows the customer best at every store. Who knows what a customer wants?

The answer is that it is the team that are customer-facing on the store floor. In which case, he said, its logical that this team decides what to stock on the shelves, how to stock on the shelves, and not some back-office purchase manager who never saw the customer. This was a revolutionary thought. He didn't just stop there.

Mackey created small teams that functioned as independent profit centers. Besides salary, the team was given a share in the profits every week as bonus, if they performed above a base threshold. The bonus was for the team, not the individual. So if one member in the team underperformed, it would affect the bonus of the whole team. The message was very clear. You decide as a team, how much you want to earn, not some HR or finance manager!

If the teams were collectively incentivized, shouldn't the teams be empowered to choose their members? Absolutely. So it was not HR that hired people but the teams collectively sat in on the decision making process. Obviously the selection was made extremely carefully, after a thorough evaluation simply because one wrong hire could cut their bonus into half!

The whole organization culture was one of celebrating teamwork. Every staff-meeting started with the members acknowledging how they delivered exceptional customer experience, thanks to the active participation not just of their own team members but cross-functional teams too, who made it possible. In fact this was celebrated in the company's mission statement as "Declaration of Interdependence" and went on to describe "Whole Foods team as a community working together to create value for others"

In order to encourage a culture of transparency, John Mackey went one step further. He put a cap on his own salary and said that at no point in time his salary will be more than 19 times the average wage (in typical fortune 500 companies, it is 1000:1).

Unlike Henry Ford who lamented: 'Why do I get a brain when I ask for a pair of hands', Whole Foods unabashedly acknowledged that the company's success depended on its employees bringing not just their body to work but their brains and heart as well.

Whole Food's culture made it possible to demonstrate that there was no conflict of interest between passion for sustainability and passion for profitability. The result was Whole Foods grew on an average 11% in topline year-on-year, tripling the industry average to revenues of $14 billion in 2014. Since its IPO in 1992, it has been the most profitable store per square foot. And quite unlike the high attrition rates that plague the retail industry, Whole Foods has stayed at a happy rate of less than 5%.

In other words, culture, like design, is not what it is but what it does!

When John Mackey started Whole Foods in 1930, it was a startup. But right from the early days, Mackey was clear that what would set his company apart from all others – not just his retail compatriots – was his unique organization culture.

So should the founding team articulate, plan and implement its organizational culture? Yes and yes and yes. Good culture does not just facilitate strategy implementation. It becomes the most powerful strategic tool in itself!

In the early days of an organization, typically, it is the personal values and management style of the founding team that constitutes culture. I must admit here that in the pre-market stage, I am not a great believer in the idea of startups not having offices and team members working out of home. I have a scientific reason for not liking it.

First of all, everyone is young and working on his own steam. There is no incentive except the intellectual challenge of the product itself. Individual energy levels are very high. The size of the team is small and the founding team is not much older or wiser than the hired teams.

Under such circumstances, pooling the energy into a physical space yields higher harnessing power. I don't have statistical evidence for this but I have plenty of anecdotal evidence to offer you – both in my own company as well as in some of my mentee companies – how productivity skyrocketed the moment we hired an office and started ideating 'physically'. At this stage, everything is on the fly and it would be a pity to miss out the excitement of the extempore! Also it is very easy to be demoralized when you are working in isolation but in a collective, you not only feed on the energy of the collective but also the unbridled optimism. So at this stage, I don't think anyone thinks about culture. Not the founders, nor the team members. The only vague reference to it is in terms of the founder's creativity.

Once the product starts to shape up and ready to be piloted, the team is suddenly exposed to the outside world. Up until now, it was operating in a controlled environment. That is when the team starts experiencing more than just the creativity of the founding team. They begin to feel the vibrations of the founding team's 'management style'. These manifest in the teams asking questions such as how willing and open are the founding members to new ideas, to failures and to accept that the team members too have brilliant ideas and give credit where it is due.

The answers to these questions, in effect, set the tone for the first cut of the company's organization culture. So culture is not something that happens on its own; it is an act of intentionally and volitionally constructing 'ways of doing things' within the organization. If you ignore culture, it will reflect in the following activities:

Hiring

At the startup stage, hiring is a process governed not by talent but by the ask rate. Since money is in short supply, the founding team hires whoever is available cheap and within their budget. If the person is talented, that's a bonus; if he is not, we will 'manage for the time being', say the founders.

Vision sharing

I have sat through plenty of recruitment interviews in startups. I have never had the privilege of witnessing the founding teams enunciate why somebody should join them. It is always transactional in that it is all laid out matter-of-factly; this is the job, this is what we expect and this is what we can pay you.

It is always such a one-sided dictum, never a conversation where the interviewee is shown the relevance of why he should join them. Just the way you have to show empathy and relevance to your customers, you have to show the same empathy and relevance to the people whom you are looking to hire.

Bad enough there is no vision sharing at the time of the interview; there is none even after the person comes on board!

Band-Aid on a festering wound

Have you noticed how most startups offer their 'startup statuses' as excuses for all bad things? Like when they can't pay the market rate; when they don't have systems and processes; when they have shabby untidy offices; when they don't practice excellence in their work ethic and when they project chaos as their value proposition!

No induction whatsoever

Bad enough the new hire has no clue to your vision. Even the way he is welcomed into the organization leaves a lot to be desired. The new team member comes in with a lot of expectation as he is joining a mint-fresh startup, thinking that he will be part of the team that will disrupt every day. That one day, when this company becomes bigger than Google, his ID card that says he is employee No. 2 will have complete auction value!

What does reality in most startups look like? A chaotic, untidy office, people screaming across the few heads that are attached to feet rolling around and somebody shoving you, saying, dude grab a table and get started! Get started on what?

No system for factoring and supporting failure

May be it is the innocence of the age, but no one in the team factors failure. I remember an incident when I first met the team of one of my mentees. My mentee invited me to address them because they were low on morale and wanted me to cheer them up. I started by saying how failure is a distinct possibility. Everyone looked at me as if I just said that I had assassinated the Pope! If your culture stigmatizes failure, no one in your organization, including you, will rise above mediocrity because you cannot create great products by being a ship that wants to say in the harbor as it is afraid of the storm on the high seas!

Blame and Fire

Not factoring failure in your scheme of things leads to a huge rollercoaster of pointing fingers, blaming someone (usually the one lowest on the totem pole), firing people, threatening them of dire consequences, not paying their dues and generally packing them off home in humiliation. I have heard entrepreneurs say that humiliation is done publicly so that it is a lesson for the other team members to deter them from failing. This is the biggest load of baloney that I have ever heard. It certainly sends one clear message home to others; they should revamp their resumes and look for a switch, pronto!

I have seen only one entrepreneur in my life who takes ownership of failure, not once but a few times. Each time, he has grown in my eyes.

None of the above behooves well for an organization that plans to grow. So who is responsible for the culture of the organization? Should one create a position of Chief Culture Officer (CCO) in the organization to create and safeguard culture?

Why not? It may not be a bad idea! Kishore Biyani hired Devdutt Pattanik, the Indian mythologist as the Chief Belief Officer of the Future Group, exactly for this reason!

But remember, even if you hire one, the fact remains that the culture of the organization is necessarily the culture of the founders. If that is good and the founders live by its code without exception, and set an example to the rest of the team, the team will have no problems adopting it as the culture of the organization. For example, NCR the company that makes ATM's was known for its sales culture and its obsession with monthly targets.

There is an apocryphal story that, during World War II, their factory in Germany had been bombed out and two men were seen walking amidst the debris. One was the CEO of NCR and the other was the local area salesman. I don't know this for a fact but it makes a good story and drives home the point I'm making, so I will share it. Apparently, the conversation between the two went something like this and I'm quoting from memory of what I read somewhere:

> CEO: You are looking worried Will, is everything ok?
> Salesman: Yes sir. But I'm thinking how will I complete my target for this month when the factory is destroyed?

> CEO: Not to worry Will, we will get the factory up and running in the next 15 days. You will have 15 more days to catch up before the month is over. Now give me a hand in rebuilding this!

NCR's sales culture came from its founder, John H. Patterson, who set up the world's first sales training school because 'we cannot afford to have a single dissatisfied customer'!

So culture necessarily is a top down artifact. I am not a subscriber to the theory that culture has to be a bottom up exercise. I don't even know how that is possible. Some people quote Toyota as an example of this and say that Toyota is successful because its production is called the 'thinking people system' where employees are encouraged to take ownership of problems and solve them.

All this tells me is that Toyota's top management has an excellent culture that encourages and incorporates recommendations and suggestions from the shop floor which in turn makes it possible to be a hugely innovative company. It tells me that culture in Toyota is top down.

Somehow entrepreneurs have underestimated the role of culture in growing their business. May be because most entrepreneurs come from an engineering background and have not studied organization behavior (now you know why I insist that every entrepreneur should do a course in OB). It does not even occur to them that notwithstanding the brilliance of their business ideas, they may not be successful if their organization culture is poor. At least I haven't heard anyone say that their company failed because they had lousy organization culture!

So what kind of culture is conducive for getting the best resources and for growing the business?

Many years ago, I remember seeing Infosys's Mission Statement (it was on the workstation of every employee, I don't know if it is still in currency). Among other things, it said, we want to build a company that employees would be proud to work in, vendors would be proud to be associated with and competitors would be proud to look up to. I had melted, I remember, at the poignancy of those words!

What kind of culture does an organization need to implement such a Mission Statement?

The answer is fairly simple, simplistic even.

Right hires

As Bill Hewlett said, hire people who want to board the bus because of who is on the bus, not because of where the bus is going!

Don't just talk of innovation

Make it your company's core competence and build systems around it. As early as 1999, Dave Whitwam, the CEO of Whirlpool told his team that since innovation was central to its leadership, he would set up processes and systems to propagate it. So he brought on board Nancy Snyder, who was the company's vice president, as the culture champion (Source of Whirlpool use case: Gary Hamel's book, *The Future of Management*). He didn't just stop there.

- ❖ He then set aside a budget for innovation,
- ❖ Trained more than 600 mentors,
- ❖ Enrolled every salaried employee in an online course on business innovation,
- ❖ Got the product department to draw up new-to-market innovation plan,

* Made innovation a large component of annual bonus,
* Reviewed on a quarterly basis each team's innovation performance,
* Set up an innovation board to fast-track ideas,
* Set up a portal to support employees with innovation tools and
* Developed a set of metrics to track innovation

Result

* By 2005, $760 million of the total revenue of $14 billion came from innovation, up from $10 million in 2001.
* 568 new products were under development, 195 of which were ready for immediate launch
* Which would in turn add another $3 billion to the company's turnover annually

---

Don't just talk. Walk the talk

No amount of preaching helps as much as the founding team demonstrating it with its own behavior. Narayan Murthy had famously said, in the early days of Infosys, that he could not have one set of rules for the founders and another for the employees. If frugality as a discipline was to be practiced in an organization, it simply meant everyone had to be frugal. It couldn't be that employees traveled by bus so that the founding team could take a flight! I know this for a fact that for many years, even after tasting success, Infosys did not allow anyone to travel executive class.

Keep them hungry

It is not enough that you, as an entrepreneur, are hungry. Your culture has to stoke that hunger in your teams so that they can make your customers hungry for your products! That's exactly what Apple does!

Earn respect

For some reason, we have forgotten this value. It is strange because in India we have always given primacy to respect, particularly for someone older and wiser. Maybe the average age of the leaders has shrunk so much that we have lost this value.

If you walk the talk, you automatically earn your team's respect. I have realized that respect and admiration forge better relationships in an organization than blind loyalty or servility.

Conversely, as an employee, being on first name terms with your boss who is the founder does not mean that you can behave 'familiarly'. Your culture should teach you how to draw the line between personal and official.

Be consistent

Nothing confuses employees more than the founding team's unpredictable behavior. For one of our mentee companies, we were interviewing a potential candidate for a senior position. He had quit a very high-paying job in an IT company that is written about in the media quite often. He had sat at home for six months before even looking for a new job. When I asked him why he quit, his answer was very strange. He said: I simply got tired of outguessing my boss every single time (he reported to one of the founders). He said his boss changed his stance so often that it seemed there was no organization culture at all!

Inspire performance

Performance is well-rounded word. It means attitude, aptitude and altitude (here it does not mean height but your generosity of spirit). Even the best run companies have appointment letters that is one long tirade of *thou shalt not!* Why don't we write positive appointment letters (let's consign all contract lawyers to hell) that inspire people to work and not turn tail?

Did you know that studies have shown that if you reward people regularly, they lose motivation? On the other hand, if you offer relevance, you don't need an HR department to motivate people (I have also never really understood how HR can motivate!). If your organization culture emphasizes competence, autonomy and purpose, you will have superlative performers.

You can inspire this not by ESOP (stock options to employees) or regular hikes in salaries and perks but reiterating to them that the work they do is game changing. Genentech, a cutting edge company involved in cancer research, creates little stories of how its research saves lives and encourages all of its employees to pin these stories on the pin-up board of their work stations. Logic? If I know how important my work is, I can keep myself inspired!

Build a company that is embracing

We see a number of acquisitions in the startup space. Many startups raise money to acquire companies and hit the accelerator. Their growth cycles are reduced phenomenally because they choose to grow inorganically. Sometimes, companies are bought solely for the talent, not so much for the product (what is called Acquihires).

Buying is an easier step. Integrating the new teams with the existing ones seamlessly is an art and it is the responsibility, not of the HR department, but of the founding team. Many a time, if cultures don't match, your investment could go down the drain. If you can make things better, make them. High performance cultures have at their core the mindset to make things better.

Let me put it simply. You quit a high paying job because you didn't like the culture of your company. Don't build an organization which has the same kind of culture that you ran away from!

Summary

Like I said before, building organization culture is a top down exercise. If that exercise is good, you build high performance teams. Performance is not just about financial metrics. It is a composite of attitude, competence, goodwill and brand equity earned in the marketplace. Remember, you are your brand's biggest ambassador. So as they say in Shakespearean plays, you have to be above suspicion like Ceasar's wife. Only then can you build a high performance organization culture.

TAKEAWAYS

- Successful organizations are those that have mastered the art of building nurturing cultures
- It is the singular responsibility of the founding team
- Cultures are dynamic entities. They evolve, adjust, recalibrate according to the needs of the organization, but their core business values remain the same
- There cannot be any conflict between personal values and business values
- Cultures have the capability to outlast organizations and entrepreneurs

Design thinking applied by
Thomas Edison in 1879.

WHAT IS DESIGN THINKING AND WHY DO YOU NEED IT AS AN ENTREPRENEUR?

> " Design is a funny word. Some people think it is how it looks. But of course if you really dig deeper, it is how it works "
>
> – Steve Jobs

WHEN I BEGAN WRITING this chapter, I was looking for a simple, non-jargonized description of what design thinking does and the insight came not from IDEO or Apple but from a family business entrepreneur, Nisa Godrej. In an interview with *The Economic Times*, she said, "we have been around for 118 years and our customers trust us. Yet we are often considered our parents' brand. Design thinking helps us be an Antevasin" (Source: *The Economic Times*, dated 29th August, 2015)

Antevasin, a Sanskrit word, pronounced as *un–teh–vaasi*. The literal meaning is, *un-teh* which means the end of boundary or border. *Vaasi* is someone who lives there. Allegorically, it means someone who has one leg this side of the border but the other leg moving towards the unknown.

The unknown here represents infinity. When does someone go live on the boundary of the forest? When he is done and dusted with living, given up everything to seek a higher purpose. In that process he has one leg still rooted in life and the other is exploring the higher purpose which is out there in infinity and yet unknown to him. That is the meaning of antevasin.

Bingo, I said. I can so relate to this. That is exactly what you do in design thinking. You know some aspects of your customer's need (as represented by the leg which is this side of the border) and there are a whole lot of things you set out to discover (as represented by the other leg which is exploring the unknown). So together, you keep pushing the boundaries.

Didn't Malcolm Gladwell call such a person an outlier (to refer to someone who thinks not within the confines of precedence and practice)? This made so much sense and this is why I wanted to write on why design thinking is necessary for entrepreneurs. Design thinking helps entrepreneurs put customers at the center of their product design, which in turn results in the most compelling user experience. This is the reason I have used Aravind Eye Care as a walk-through validation of design thinking in this chapter.

You will find, throughout this book, a constant reference to user experience and empathy for users. Design thinking not only celebrates this but also helps you weave it into your organization culture. So what is design thinking?

One of the things I have said again and again in this book is that there are two kinds of entrepreneurs; the ones who see a problem and design a solution to fix the problem, thereby improving life. The others are those who design a solution for improving life even before something becomes a problem.

In the first, he's addressing a need; in the second, he's addressing something before it became a need. Once he addresses it, if the solution is taken away, it becomes a palpable need.

Simple examples to explain both are: day travelers felt the need for convenient single use disposable toothpaste. Colgate designed Wisp, and added an element of surprise to it. Wisp was not just a small tube but came with a small toothbrush as well. He brushed and he disposed both the toothbrush and the toothpaste. The day traveler's need was met.

Facebook is a good example of unfelt need but now that we have it, we can't imagine life without it.

In both the examples, the user was at the center of the universe. In designing a compelling experience for him, you are in a position to see the problem not only in a new light but in its totality. So the solution you come up with is not piecemeal but a wholesome one. Let us look at a use case of Aravind Eye Care, headquartered in Madurai, to understand this.

Dr G.Venkataswamy set out to address one specific problem in India – cataract blindness. His concern was that there were nine million cataract patients who would go blind if untreated. The reason many of them would go blind was because cataract surgery was very expensive and therefore many of the patients may not go for surgery. Now let us break this up into probing questions and see how design thinking aided Dr G, as he is known, in addressing this.

First level of the problem:

Why is cataract surgery expensive?
Because the ocular lens is expensive

Why is the ocular lens expensive?
Because it is imported

How expensive is it?
It costs $100 a piece

Solution

We should stop importing and start manufacturing ocular lenses in India.

Second level of the problem

If we set up manufacturing in India, we can bring down the cost of the ocular lens to $2 a piece. Then the cost of the surgery can be brought down from Rs 30, 000 to Rs. 5000. More people can afford it.

But not all can afford it.

For those who cannot afford it, we should do the surgery free.

So, should we charge more for those who can afford so that they subsidize the cost of those who can't?

No, that would be unfair.

Then where will we get the money to pay for the surgeries of the poor? Should we seek donation?

No, because donation is not a certainty. The day donations stop, do we have to stop surgeries?

Not at all.

Then what else can we do?

Solution

We could export ocular lenses and earn revenue.

Third level of the problem

How about bringing down other costs as well so that we can not only do free surgery for the poor but we also don't overcharge those who can afford to pay?

Like what?

Why can't we do more surgeries per day?

We can't because number of operation theatres is finite and number of eye surgeons is limited.

Suppose we increase the number of surgeries without increasing the number of OT's or eye surgeons?

How?

Suppose we McDonald-ize surgeries.

Huh?

You have seen how process-driven it is in a McDonald outlet, right, from order taking to fulfillment?

Yes.

Suppose we do the same.
How?

Tell me, how long does a cataract surgery take in the OT?
15 minutes.

What is the process in these 15 minutes?
There is pre-surgery prepping (hydrating the eye), surgery (which is fitting the ocular lens) and post-surgery.

Do you need the eye surgeon in the entire process?
No, only when the ocular lens is fitted.

How long does it take for the eye surgeon to fit the lens?
Two minutes.

So out of 15 minutes surgery, you need the eye surgeon only for two minutes?
Yes

Well-trained Para medical staff can manage the balance 13 minutes?
Of course, they are doing it even now.

Right now we have one patient per OT at a time?
Yes

Suppose we lined up in a row, several patients in the OT at various stages of the surgery. Let us say, we line up 10 patients. Three of them are being prepped for surgery, three are having their lens fitted and the rest are in post-surgery.
That means Paras are managing seven patients and doctors are administering three.

To manage seven patients at a time, how many Paras do you need?

Two, as they are all next to each other.

To fit the ocular lens in three patients, how many eye surgeons do you need?

You need one, because he can do one after the other in quick succession.

So if one eye surgeon can manage three patients in six minutes, how many surgeries can he do in a 6-hour shift?

180 surgeries (6 hours = 360 minutes/2 = 180)

Typically how many surgeries does an eye surgeon perform now?

Six

So if we have a process that makes him perform even 100 surgeries per day, do we still need more eye surgeons?

No.

Solution

So we cut down costs by improving efficiency of the eye surgeons (by adopting processes that increases systemic efficiency and improving human productivity).

Similarly, if one OT can take 10 patients at a time and, in a 20-hour cycle, it can take how many patients?

600 patients (20 hours x60mins/2=600)

So even if we perform 500 surgeries per day, do we need more OT's?

No.

Solution

Similarly cut down infrastructural costs by optimizing OT occupancy.

Fourth level of the problem

What other costs can we reduce?

Why use iron stretchers? Tamil Nadu is full of bamboo forests. Why not make bamboo stretchers? They are lighter and cheaper.

Solution

We can further cut down costs by replacing iron stretchers with bamboo ones.

Fifth level of the problem

Now we need more trained Para medical staff.

We won't get Para medical staff readymade.

We can hire 10th standard pass from the towns and villages of Tamil Nadu.

We can set up a training school and train them.

Solution

So in one shot we create skilled labor and provide employment.

Sixth level of the problem

Since we have a training school for training Para medical staff, why not place them in other hospitals for a small fee? Yes.

Solution

We can also do body shopping to overseas markets where there is a huge demand for such people for a fee.

Seventh level of the problem:

Tamil Nadu is a big state. How do we reach out to every cataract patient who lives in far-flung villages?

Contact the local Panchayats. Install webcams in strategic locations. Diagnose on the webcam their criticality. Organize buses on a given day to gather all the patients together and bring them to the Madurai hospital for treatment. The patient can be discharged within hours of the surgery.

Solution

Optimal reach by online diagnosis and by collective transport to hospital.

Eighth level of problem

But the patient can't come alone. His caregiver will also accompany him.

No problem.

Solution

We will build a dormitory for the caregivers.

Thus Dr G came up with a solution to a problem called cataract blindness by bringing down the cost of surgery in the most holistic manner possible. His design thinking resulted in:

- ❖ Stopping import of ocular lenses at $100 dollar a piece, manufacturing it locally at $2 apiece and exporting it at $50 apiece to all parts of the world (India is the largest exporter of ocular lenses today)

- ❖ Cutting down resource costs by improving productivity of eye surgeons

- ❖ Cutting down infrastructural cost by optimizing OT occupancy

- ❖ Cutting down costs by replacing iron stretchers with bamboo (this is a very important element of design thinking that you don't ignore any aspect of the problem, however small it is)

- ❖ Up-skilling the youth from the hinterland of Tamil Nadu (and now Andhra Pradesh, Kerala and Karnataka) and creating employment opportunities

- ❖ Body shopping of trained paramedical staff to overseas markets

- ❖ Optimizing reach through online diagnosis and transporting them as a collective to the hospital

- ❖ Dormitory for caregivers

All of this resulted in Dr G building a charity eye hospital with 300 percent RoI (return on investment.). That is the power of design thinking.

And India did not wake up to this wonderful brand in its backyard until HBR showcased it and Dr C.K.Prahlad visited it!

Design-thinking as you have seen from the above example is a creative and systematic approach to problem solving, by putting your user at the center of the experience. It is not about what you want as an entrepreneur. It is what you visualize best for your customer; jointly with your customer as a fellow conspirator in the process. (I am using the word conspirator as opposed to partner here because, to my mind, it is a beautifully invested word. It suggests that as an entrepreneur, you are not working in isolation, but making customer your fellow designer and between the two of you, a magical experience is designed for him).

So there may be some needs that your customer may be able to feel and articulate. There may be some needs that you may foresee and gently nudge the customer into seeing them too. And there may be some that you both discover along the way, serendipitously.

Summary

Design thinking is an imperative journey for you, the entrepreneur and your team to stay relevant in the marketplace. It should become embedded in your organization culture.

The elements of design thinking are framing the problem, empathizing with the customer, integrating all aspects of the solution and igniting the imagination of your customer!

TAKEAWAYS

- Design thinking is a thought, a doctrine, a commitment, a *junoon* (Urdu word for passion), and a way of lofty living (as opposed to a mediocre or mundane living)

- It is not just a survival imperative. It has a more exalted goal of staying connected with your customer at every level and at all times

- It is good to adopt design thinking as the framework in which your organization operates because that way you will always stay reinvented!

- It should become the DNA that underwrites your organizational culture

SUTRA X

WHO ARE THE
INVESTORS?

> **"** Be fearful when others are greedy.
> Be greedy when others are fearful **"**
>
> – Warren Buffett

GOING BY THE EXTRAORDINARILY high glamour quotient of the investors in the entrepreneurial ecosystem, you'd be tempted to think that investor belongs to a new species that has made its appearance, along with the new age entrepreneur. The truth is the investor preceded the animal called entrepreneur!

Seafarer and the investor

When the seafaring bug bit someone in the 11th or 12th century, the first person the explorer sought was an investor, who would bankroll his madness. There was no Microsoft those days, so obviously no major resource estimation on elaborate spreadsheets happened.

I'm not even sure a back-of-the-envelope calculation was *de rigueur* in those days. I guess it was a simple transaction in a watering hole between the investor and the seafarer where the latter named the first biggest number that popped literally from his hat and the investor, depending on his own grasp of the number, either agreed or chopped.

In return, the seafarer promised three things- a percentage of revenue from the sale of goodies that the ship carried, some of the goodies themselves (silk and spice for instance were in huge demand, sometimes human slaves also came with the pack) and a marking on the hull of the ship that Mr. X is the captain of the ship and Mr. Y is the investor who made it possible.

I have read stories about how intense negotiation would be centered, not around the RoI (return on investment), but on the size of the lettering of the investor's name on the plaque of the ship which carried the vessel's name, and that of its captain's.

Another business that sprung around this time was insurance. It was the insurer who underwrote the investment in the seafarer's adventure! So as early as 11th century, not only were the investor and insurer well entrenched in business but they guarded their turf by putting a mechanism in place that mitigated the risks!

Inventions and the investor

By the time the cotton-ginning machine was invented by Eli Whitney in mid-1750, the investment climate was fairly conducive. Although the definition of the word 'entrepreneur' underwent significant changes through history, the resource management aspect of an entrepreneur's role always had primacy over everything else.

During the 18th century, when large-scale construction of churches and abbeys were happening in Europe, the on-site manager came to be known as an entrepreneur because it was his primary responsibility to manage the resources, on site, judiciously and optimally.

Debt Investor

By mid-20th century, investment became synonymous with loans. Since banking institutions were developed by then, one of their services was collateralized lending. A number of rich businessmen also lent money for business, even if Shylock gave them all a bad name.

As a result, the manufacturing sector throve on the model of debt financing. In most societies, banks were set up to offer debt financing as one of their high visibility products. The banks, with their disdain for risk, perfected the model over time.

The steps involved were as follows: the businessman, (not the 'entrepreneur' mind you, that epithet came in vogue along with the internet) submitted a project proposal to the bank, outlining details about his product, the industry, his customer profile, and the financials which included how much money he needs, for what and how much he will make and when. It also included details of the collateral the businessman was willing to offer against the loan.

Typically, the collateral was in the form of some immovable property, but other assets such as gold jewelry, government bonds, gilt-edge shares and debentures were also acceptable. The bank assigned a project manager to go over the proposal, evaluate the risks (not just business related risks but also businessman related. His reputation, credibility, his affiliations and standing in society were the chief markers. In fact, it wasn't unheard of for a businessman to say 'I m a Rotarian' as proof of his credentials!

I have been told that in the good old days, outside State Bank of India's zonal offices, which were responsible for disbursing loans to businesses, a typical fixture would be a steno-typist with a Facit or Remington manual typewriter. He was a man much in demand because he not only had the template for the project proposal that was required to be submitted to the bank, but over the years had acquired a certain amount of understanding of what catches the attention of the loan manager. Accordingly he would suggest to the businessman to ask for more loan or tone down the sales projection or pad up the profit margin!

But this whole business of getting loan from a bank was a long-drawn process where your personal relationship with the bank may fetch you some brownie points but it was largely a cumbersome, involved, time-consuming and anxiety-inducing exercise.

The only alternative to this was to approach the moneylender who did not ask too many uncomfortable questions but he demanded several pounds of flesh by way of a prohibitive interest on the loan.

If the amount required was smaller and you had rich and influential friends and family, you could tap them for a loan. If the requirement was large you had no option but to approach the bank.

The loans were disbursed at a pre-determined interest rate. The loan period was also pretty much pre-determined although, depending on the clout of the businessman, there was some room for negotiation here. You could also get a moratorium or repayment holiday for a brief period. For example, you could ask for a waiver of loan repayment for the first six months on the ground that you would need four months for your production to commence and a buffer of two months would be very nice, thank you.

The biggest upside of debt is that your equity is safe and the process of repaying the loan – both principal and interest – inculcates a fiscal discipline in you, which stands you in good stead.

The biggest downside of debt is that it is a huge drain on your cash flow, especially in the early stages of the company.

Equity Investor

Equity capital, unlike debt, is not a loan that needs to be repaid, month on month, hence it does not have to be factored into the monthly cash flow. It is capital that is attracted by inviting the investor to own some part of the future growth potential of the business. In other words, it is risk capital, that is, the investor decides to buy into the growth story of the business, invests in it to contribute to and participate in it, so that in three to five years' time, it yields good return on his investment.

But the investor also knows that if the growth story does not happen, his investment could go south and since it is not a loan, it is not incumbent on the entrepreneur to return his investment. And typically, according to RoC (Registrar of Companies) bankruptcy norms, in the event a private limited company folds up, the priority payments, after salvaging from whatever saleable assets the company may have, would be towards statutory liability, employee salaries, vendor payments, the investor – necessarily in that order. Most often, there is nothing much left in the company after statutory payments.

Investing against equity or stake in the company is a relatively new phenomenon that emerged in North America when the super market culture grabbed the imagination of post war, cash-rich, consumption-hungry Americans but undoubtedly it is the Silicon Valley that gave it form, substance and impetus.

It was the Internet boom that created a whole new industry of investors. During the dotcom boom in the late 90's, the investors saw a huge opportunity, as the Internet business model was dramatically different from the brick-and-mortar model of the manufacturing sector that was in vogue until then.

What caught the eye of the investors in the early days of the Internet was the dream combination of low investment with high and speedy return. If you invested in a manufacturing business, let's say, making picture tubes for the television industry, the investment required ran into crores. It took two years for the manufacturing facility to be up and running. It took another three years to gain foothold in the market. It took three more years to become profitable. It would take at least another three years before the investor could exit profitably.

So the investment was stuck for over ten years before it could yield and in those ten years, any change in the external environment – change in government policy, natural calamities, man-made disasters such as war and terrorism, unstable currency, economic chaos induced by the collapse of financial institutions – would derail it further.

Investment in Internet companies seemed a cakewalk, in comparison. The ticket size (capital required) was smaller. It could be released in tranches linked to performance milestones. For example, let us say, an investor invested seed capital of a crore, in a start-up, for 20% stake in the company.

It is not that he was expected to write a single check of a crore, as soon as the term sheet was signed. He could specify that at the time of signing the term sheet, he would hand over a check of Rs. 25 lakhs, which would be used for customer acquisition. When the company acquired its first 50 customers (assuming it is a B2C product), the next tranche of Rs. 50 lakhs would be released so that new teams for marketing and delivery could be hired, to build traction in customer acquisition.

With this tranche, the investor may suggest that the company should be able to build enough visibility, so as to acquire maybe the next 100 customers. And the last tranche may be released once the investor gains confidence that the company is indeed implementing its business plan.

The whole objective of the exercise was that since this was risk capital, there were steps that needed to be taken to manage those risks.

Every equity investor knowingly takes risks with the hope that out of 10 investment choices that he makes, may be at least one will be a runaway success.

Typically in a basket of 10 equity investments, 3 may have some reasonable success, nothing great, the investor may not gain huge returns or even returns as expected but he may not lose his investment. 2 are likely to be duds, where the investment will have to be written off. 3 may be slow-starters, so if the investor had planned to exit in three years time, it may not happen. So either by pivoting or changing the business model dramatically after going to market, the company may see some traction, but after losing considerable amount of time. Depending on his confidence in the founding team, the investor may decide to stay on longer term and reap the benefits or cut short his losses and exit sooner. 1 may do as per the business plan and stay pretty much on track. 1 may be a runaway success. Or at least the investor prays for it to be! He pins all his hopes on the one that may throw a huge surprise by not just living up to its potential but gathering more and more momentum by way of new potential along the way. Such a start-up is known as a 'gazelle'. So, how can an investor spot one, hopefully without binoculars?

In the jungle, a gazelle (deer family) is known for its swiftness, which is the result of its 'stotting' technique. When a predator is at its heels, initially, the gazelle runs at an even pace, and then unexpectedly, she lifts all four feet and jumps high into the air, and then flees, thereby leaving the predator clueless and frustrated. This is called stotting.

In entrepreneurship, a gazelle is a start-up, which has grown swiftly. A gazelle is the embodiment of the fast and the furious. It takes off with such alacrity in a short span of time that it leaves competitors burnt and hapless.

Is there a way one can spot a gazelle even before it becomes one? Or does it always have to be post fact? My take is that, as in most things in life, nothing happens overnight. The signals and symptoms are all there, you just need a powerful Maglite to spot them.

So what are the symptoms the investors should look for? Here are some, and by no means is this an exhaustive list!

- ❖ A 'chameleonic' quality in the entrepreneur: Let's say an entrepreneur has invested time, effort and money into developing a product. He goes to market and discovers that there is another opportunity in the same space, which is bigger by way of market size, faster by way of monetization and traction, and significantly better, by way of improving lives

- ❖ The litmus test is, will the entrepreneur dither in the face of opportunity, even turn away from it saying he cannot start from ground up all over again, or will he abandon the original idea and tailgate on the new one? Will he treat the time spent on the first as part of the learning curve instead of lamenting that it is time lost? If the answer is that he will go after the new opportunity, chances are, you have found your gazelle

- ❖ InMobi is a good example of what I'm talking about. This Bangalore-based company started its operations in 2007 as an SMS-based mobile advertising network. A few months into the market showed them the potential of the mobile web ecosystem

❖ It was a tough call for the founding team to abandon their original product and start developing the new one, which showed so much more promise. They made the call and today, InMobi is the second largest independent mobile advertising network in the world, with 400 million customers, in over 165 countries, through more than 50 billion mobile ad impressions monthly. Wow! What a splendid gazelle indeed. And who spotted it? Marquee investors like Kleiner Perkins and Sherpalo

❖ No cut-paste please! Is the entrepreneur so clued in to his market that even if he has borrowed an idea from elsewhere, he will adapt it to his cultural context? Look at any domain today; businesses that are successful are those, which gave primacy to 'home-grown-ness'

❖ The New Delhi-based Snapdeal illustrates this very well. It started in February 2010 as a daily deals platform like Groupon, but expanded in September 2011 to become the second largest e-commerce company in India

❖ The investors who spotted this gazelle early enough are Nexus Venture Partners and Indo-US Ventures and Snapdeal since then has raised several more rounds of capital

❖ Magic carpet! Is the entrepreneur excited only by his idea or has he woven all the nuances of taking his idea to the market, clearly, flawlessly, and magically into a beautiful business model that makes sense?

❖ Flipkart, the Bangalore based company, is an excellent example of this. The two Bansals, who are not related to each other, but are co-founders, not only were passionate about bringing to India, the Amazon model,but were serious about delighting the customer, end to end – from product discovery to fulfillment

❖ Flipkart not only sells a whole range of products (although they started with only books) but it is also almost as ruthlessly efficient as Wal-Mart in its backend management and logistics

❖ Flipkart started towards end 2007, has been growing 100% every quarter, and it was India's first billion-dollar Internet start-up, after several rounds of funding! And the first to spot the potential was Accel India and subsequently, Tiger Global. An interesting fact is that both these investors have not only stayed invested in Flipkart, they even participated in a fresh round of funding of $ 1 billion in 2013!

❖ K.I.S.S (Keep it simple, stupid!) Is the business idea simple, low on initial capex, high on potential and market reach? If the answer is yes to all, you have found your gazelle yet again

❖ The US based Dropbox, was founded in 2007 with the idea of doing away with the inconvenience of managing data from multiple computers. It is a very simple web based file hosting service that uses cloud computing so that users can store and share files and folders with each other. When one of the founders first demonstrated it at MIT, someone in the audience asked him: "It is such a simple idea, how come no one thought of it before?"

❖ Y Combinator's Paul Graham was the first investor. In 2011, Dropbox raised $250 million from marquee investors such as Index Ventures, Greylock, Sequoia, Benchmark, Accel, Goldman Sachs, and RIT Capital Partners at a valuation of $ 4 billion

Enterprises that are adaptable, that show preference to home grown ideas, that are passionate not just about ideas but their execution too, and embrace simplicity as a virtue are all huge potential gazelles.

Dear investor, see a gazelle stotting away at a distance? Catch her before someone else does!

Like I said earlier, every investor hopes to invest in one gazelle at least, in his lifetime.

Who are the Angels and the Venture Capitalists? (VC's)?

Angels typically are investors who come in at a very early stage in the life of a startup, pre-market or just after going to market. The average investment is in the range of Rs.25 lakhs to a crore and the investment is made against equity.

The angels could be individuals from the entrepreneur's network, what in common parlance is called the three F's – friends, family and fools. In India, the three F's also mean friends, family and father-in-law.

Such investors are called angels because they show confidence in the entrepreneur when he is not able to demonstrate even a minimum viable product (MVP). This confidence stems largely from their familiarity with the entrepreneur and his family members. So they fund the entrepreneur, not so much his business.

The angels could also be from an organized consortium of entrepreneurs and investors such as the Indian Angel Network (IAN). IAN has several chapters across metros and they do open house with entrepreneurs regularly to scout for good business ideas. Angels mostly fund seed capital. Very rarely do they venture into growth capital funding.

Up until three years ago, the venture capitalists or VC's as they are known (some uncharitable entrepreneurs also call them vulture capitalists, I don't need to explain why!), came from the BFSI domain (banking, financial services and insurance). They had work experience in this domain in India and overseas. Either they continued to work for large VC firms or started off on their own, having seen the exploding opportunity in India. According to yourstory.in, the top 15 investors in Indian start-ups in January-June 2015, and I quote from the article, are:

"Investors focused on Indian startups have been a busy lot this year. They have closed 380 deals between January and June 2015, compared to 304 deals in 2014.

With Internet and mobile continuing to dominate, it is not surprising that technology-focused investors make up most of our list of Top Investors according to deal numbers.

Sequoia Capital India, which raised its fourth India-focused fund worth $530 million last year, heads the list with 26 deals.

The US-based Tiger Global Management, which almost single-handedly sparked the e-commerce fund rush in India, made 20 investments in the first half of the year. Tied at the second spot is Helion Venture Partners with SAIF Partners rounding up the top three with 18 deals".

But one interesting trend that has emerged in the last three years is that successful entrepreneurs are investing in start-ups either through their companies or in their personal capacity.

Paytm for instance has invested twice in Jugnoo, a Chandigarh-based online aggregator for autorickshaw rides. Ratan Tata has invested in a wide range of hot sectors, ranging from jewelry (Bluestone) furniture (Urban Ladder), online wallet (Paytm), clean energy (Altaeros), auto classified (Cardekho), data-driven research platform (Tracxn) and healthcare (Swasth India). Till date, he has invested in 10 startups and the investment ranges from Rs 1 to 5 crores in each of them. Sanjeev Kapoor, of Khana Khazana (culinary show on television) fame and the founder of Wonderchef, invested in a startup called ZuperMeal, which is a mobile aggregator of home-cooked meals.

Similarly companies such as Flipkart, Snapdeal, Practo and Ola have been investing in or buying startups. Tanuj Mendiratta sold his mobile marketing company, Appiterate, to Flipkart in in early 2015.

TOP INVESTORS (JANUARY - JUNE 2015)

NAME OF INVESTOR	NO. OF DEALS
SEQUOIA	26*
TIGER	20*
helion	20**
SAIF Partners	18
ACCEL PARTNERS	17
IndiaQuotient	16
matrix	15**
IDG Ventures India	14**
kalaari	13
NEXUS	10***

Source: Article dated 4th July 2015 in yourstory.in by Radhika Nair

Most of the well-funded companies, particularly in the Internet space have either taken majority stake in startups whose products enhance their own market reach or help them diversify into a related area. This emerging M&A strategy also gives a viable exit option to investors helping them to realize value much faster.

Debt Investors

It is a well-known truism that commercial banks do not understand the Internet business model and have therefore steered clear of lending money to startups. Keeping this in mind, a number of online consumer lending portals have sprung up that offer P2P lending. In 2013, there were 2 such portals. In 2015, there were 22. Investors who obviously don't see much risk in this model have backed many of them.

Prominent among them are IndiaLends, InstaPaisa, InstaKash, LendBox, LoanStreet, Loan Circle, and LoanMeet. All of them offer personal loans, some of them even offer business loans and their biggest value proposition is that they process the loan application online, and in 24 hours.

The Internet platform aggregates lenders and borrowers. The huge plus of this model for lenders is that "they get high risk adjusted returns as rates are calculated on borrower's credit profile. (Similarly) the borrowers get loans at rates more attractive than the banks, it is online, transparent and quick funding" (Source: *The Economic Times Magazine*, dated November 15-21, 2015) the amounts typically are under Rs 10 lakhs.

Since these are new startups, it is yet to be assessed how good the recovery rate is.

Sachet Investors

The aura around billion dollar valuations and the whole buzz created around entrepreneurship has given rise to a new class of investors. I call them 'sachet investors'. Let's say you work as VP Projects in TCS. Let's say your cost-to-company is Rs 50 lakhs per annum and out of this you are easily able to set aside Rs 25 lakhs for investments. Up until 3 years ago, your options for investing your savings from salary were limited to low risk, low yield government bonds, recurring deposits in banks, real estate, gold, and mutual funds, both debt and equity based. Or you could invest in companies by buying their shares on the stock market. But this was possible only if they were public limited companies.

But thanks to the start-up ecosystem, you now have yet another option and an exciting one at that. You could do this either through your network or there are fund managers who mobilize part of your savings into investing in startups.

Let's say a startup needs Rs.25 lakhs seed money to take their product to market. One option they have is to borrow this money from their own network of the three Fs – friends, family and fools (in India it is also known as friends, family and father-in-laws!). Let's say for this they are prepared to give up 25% stake.

The second option they have is sachetized capital. They may raise Rs. 2.5 lakhs each from 10 different investors to raise the same Rs. 25 lakhs by giving each investor 1% equity in the company, that is, they have raised Rs. 25 lakhs for a total of 10% stake.

One obvious benefit of this move is that they have parted with lesser equity. But the bigger benefit is that since the ten investors hold only 1% each in the company, no one has any major control of the company. No one can tell the entrepreneur how he should build his company and this freedom is very important for the entrepreneur – the freedom to implement his vision. Just because someone has invested in his company, he can't allow him to hijack his vision and hold him to ransom!

An emerging form of sachetized capital is crowdfunding which uses the Internet to create a platform for mobilizing small investments from investors who are not professional investment agencies or organizations but are individuals who see this kind of avenue as another investment opportunity.

Impact Investors

Typically these investors invest only in social ventures or what are known as Triple Bottom line Ventures (TBL). These may be for profit, not for profit and government-supported initiatives, TBL was a term coined by John Elkington and it referred to 'an accounting framework which looked beyond the traditional measures of profits, return on investment and shareholder value to include environmental and social dimensions' (Source: undated article by Timothy F. Slaper in *Indiana Business Review*, digital copy).

Impact investments, which are in organizations centered around social causes (typical ones like rural healthcare, primary education, rehabilitation of devdasis, educating the girl child, skilling rural youth, opening of bank accounts for people at the bottom of the pyramid, etc.) are gaining momentum. There are even Impactcapital exchanges set up (http://www.asiaiix.com/mission/) expressly for this purpose.

The types of investors discussed in this chapter are in the context of Internet entrepreneurs. Equity is more in vogue especially as growth capital largely because banks do not lend to Internet startups as they do not understand the business model of these companies.

For brick-and-mortar companies, more debt options are

available, fewer equity. Typical debt options are nationalized banks, SIDBI (Small Industries Development Bank of India), and SFC (State Finance Corporations). There are also government schemes announced from time to time that are industry specific.

Summary

In an ideal world, both entrepreneurs and investors should be able to exercise choice. So far in India, it is a luxury only investors have and entrepreneurs have generally displayed desperation at the negotiation table and have always had a losing hand. But it is heart-warming to note that of late, entrepreneurs too are doing due diligence on investors, some are even walking away from unattractive deals, or renegotiating deals.

TAKEAWAYS

- Choosing your investor is as important a decision as choosing your customer or your co-founder. Choose for the right reason and one that will stand in good stead both in the long term and short term

- Your goal should be to become a great company, not a unicorn. Don't fall into this valuation trap and short-change yourself

- Investors are an integral part of your ecosystem, bring them on board to strengthen your company and disrupt the world, not to go on an ego trip

SUTRA XI

WHAT ARE THE TYPES OF EQUITY INVESTMENTS?

> " Rule No.1: Never lose money.
> Rule No. 2: Never forget Rule No.1 "
>
> – Warren Buffett

BROADLY EQUITY INVESTMENTS may be classified as seed or early stage capital and growth capital. Let us see each of them in detail.

Seed Capital

Seed capital is an early stage fund and its ticket size is small. More often than not, an entrepreneur, who has just gone to market, or is about to go to market, raises seed capital. His product is ready and he raises seed capital for creating awareness about his product to his potential customer and acquiring that customer. In such cases, the seed capital may be anywhere between Rs 50 lakhs to a crore.

In some rare cases, it may be raised in the pre-market phase itself, on the strength of a proto-type. In extremely rare cases, it may even be raised for developing the prototype. In such cases, the seed capital may not be more than Rs 25 lakhs.

Normally, a college incubator or a business accelerator offers seed capital either for prototype development or in the pre-market phase, but the amount may not be more than Rs 5 lakhs.

The valuation, in all of the above cases, is arbitrary and one-sided. The investor is interested in investing at this stage simply because he can walk away with peanut valuation. He is simply looking for the 'early bird' advantage and since there is no product, no customer, and no team, scientific principles of valuation cannot be applied.

It just depends on who blinks first at the negotiation table. And in my experience, it is mostly the entrepreneur who blinks first, showing his desperation for the money, thereby throwing away any possibility of a favorable negotiation. I have known entrepreneurs who have given away 45% stake for a crore's investment and I don't know whether their hearts bled, but mine certainly did!

Growth Capital

As the name suggests, this is capital raised by the entrepreneur when he is about to hit the growth trajectory. The product is in place and has found acceptance in the market; the team is hired and is raring to go and there is a small but growing tribe of customers who have not only begun to use the product but have started talking about how it has made their life easy to their friends, on social media, in party conversations and in peer-to-peer interactions.

The conversations could be something like this: two friends meet for a cuppa, one is late and he apologizes saying, 'Sorry *yaar*, I was waiting for the carpenter and the bugger never turned up'. The other guy says: 'why don't you download the Urbanclap app, you can get just about any service from them – and they are punctual too'!

This is the moment you are ready for what is called Series A funding, which is your first fund raised from investors who are called venture capitalists or VC's as they are known in the entrepreneurial community.

VC's are those whose profession it is to make money work for them. Please see the diagram below which was enunciated by Robert Kiyosaki in his now famous book *Rich Dad, Poor Dad*.

CASHFLOW QUADRANT
4 WAYS TO PRODUCE INCOME
LINEAR INCOME VS LEVERAGED & RESIDUAL INCOME

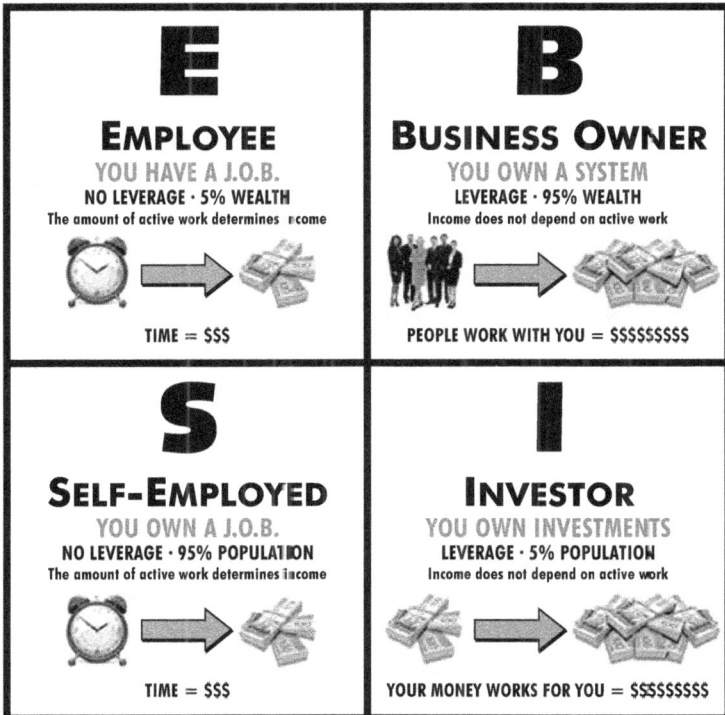

E

EMPLOYEE
YOU HAVE A J.O.B.
NO LEVERAGE · 5% WEALTH
The amount of active work determines income

TIME = $$$

B

BUSINESS OWNER
YOU OWN A SYSTEM
LEVERAGE · 95% WEALTH
Income does not depend on active work

PEOPLE WORK WITH YOU = $$$$$$$$$

S

SELF-EMPLOYED
YOU OWN A J.O.B.
NO LEVERAGE · 95% POPULATION
The amount of active work determines income

TIME = $$$

I

INVESTOR
YOU OWN INVESTMENTS
LEVERAGE · 5% POPULATION
Income does not depend on active work

YOUR MONEY WORKS FOR YOU = $$$$$$$$$

The Cash Flow Quadrant is an important diagram presented and explained by Robert Kiyosaki:

"There was an important diagram my rich dad showed me when I was a little boy. It was a diagram known as the Cash Flow Quadrant. And the Quadrant is made of four different people who make of the business world.

So my rich dad said, "In the business world there are E's and E stands for employees. And the employees, you can always tell who they are by their core values. An employee with the president, the generator of the company, will always say the same words. The words are, 'I'm looking for a safe, secure job with benefits'. That's what makes them employees because their core value is security.

The other one of the four is the S for the small business owner or the self-employed and again their core values will cause them to use the same words which are, "If you want it done right, do it by yourself." S means they are also solo. Generally a one-person act, they operate by themselves.

On the right side of the Cash Flow Quadrant are the B's. And my rich dad said, the B stood for big business, or like Bill Gates. For the B's define big business as 500 employees or more. And their words are different.

They'll say, 'I'm looking for good system, good network and the smartest people I know to help run my business.' Unlike the S, they don't want to run the company by themselves. They want smart people run the company for them.

And then, the fourth of the Cash Flow Quadrant is the I. And the I stands for the investor. These are people who have money work hard for them. These people in the B Quadrant have people work hard for them. And these people in the E & S Quadrant are the people who work hard for the rich here in the right side of the Cash Flow Quadrant, for the B's and I's".

(Quoted from Robert Kiyosaki's *Rich Dad, Poor Dad*).

So the VC's are the fourth quadrant, the investors, who make money work hard for them. They do this by investing in potential companies to fuel the growth of that company. In return for their investment, they take a stake in the company so that they can participate in the growth of the company with legitimate ownership.

The first time you raise money from VC's is called Series A funding. The minimum ticket size is $ 5 million, and although there is no upper limit as such, the fledgling company may not be in a position to demonstrate ability to absorb more capital than $ 5 million.

The normal practice is that the entrepreneur will raise $ 5-10 million from one VC only and if he needs more capital, he may shop around for more than one VC. He may even stagger fund-raising in Series A, that is, after raising $ 5 million from one investor, in less than 4 months, he may shop around for another investor for a similar amount or more. He may do this for three reasons.

❖ The entrepreneur may want to bring a strategic investor on board who will not only bring capital to the table but very valuable network as well

❖ He may not be interested in putting all his eggs in one basket

❖ The current investor may have turned him down for more money

Typically Series A fund should last for 12 to 18 months at least after deployment. If the funds are deployed as per the business plan and the company hits the growth trajectory, they may run out of capital in less than 2 years and may start shopping for capital again. This is a very happy scenario for the entrepreneur and the investor.

Series B funds are what the entrepreneur will look for once he exhausts his Series A fund. This, in my experience, is the hardest to raise. The reason is very simple.

When the entrepreneur approaches an investor for seed capital, what he's peddling is hope. When he approaches an investor for Series A fund, he's peddling his vision.

But when it comes to Series B fund, it is all on actuals-his performance report card.

If the report card is good and the Series A investor can get an exit with Series B funding, then god is in heaven and all is wonderful in the entrepreneurial world! If the magical numbers have not happened, for whatever reason, it is very hard to explain to the Series B investor without sounding whiny. This is the beginning of the end for many companies. To my mind, if an entrepreneur can navigate this one smoothly, he can pretty much be assured of longevity in the business.

Once the entrepreneur raises series A, thereafter every time he goes shopping for capital, he is shopping for growth capital only.

Valuation

Like I said, there is no science to valuing a company for seed capital, in the pre-market or just-gone-to-market stage. It could be as low as Rs 1 crore and as high as Rs 5 crores, depending on the product, industry and the competence and experience of the founding team. It is more an exercise of thumb rule and precedence. So typically when you are looking for seed capital, it is a double whammy of low valuation, high stake. The entrepreneur rarely has any bargaining power.

But in the growth phase, whilst the entrepreneur is still at the receiving end, he has a lot more flexibility in spinning his story. But it is a known fact that entrepreneurs value their company high and investors value them low and rarely do the twain meet without high-intensity negotiation at the deal table.

But of late, one has seen the emergence of a new trend, particularly in the ecommerce space where both entrepreneurs and investors are aligned to seemingly high valuation, veering towards the unreasonable at times. The fact that many of these companies are seeking high valuation based on revenue and not profit (many of the unicorns have not been profitable at all) and investors are playing along with it has done two things. Firstly it has made entrepreneurship, particularly ecommerce, hugely attractive to aspiring entrepreneurs and secondly, it has created a feeding frenzy among investors to be the first on the scene and exit with the ripest of pickings.

Summary

Choosing the right *type* of investment is as important as choosing the right *time* for investment and the right *reason* for the investment choice. Exercise caution, be cool, and decide rationally, not emotionally.

TAKEAWAYS

- Capital is the oxygen of every business and therefore it is important for the entrepreneur to factor all possible ramifications before he makes his choice

- Investors should be brought on board not just for their capital but for their knowledge and network as well

- Raising capital is a full time exercise. You can either raise capital or run the company. You can't do both. So if there are multiple co-founders, it is good to assign capital-raising responsibility exclusively to one co-founder, whilst the other continues to run the company

- Make sure your documentation is word-perfect before you get an investor on board. It is very important that you engage a contract lawyer to validate every single clause in the document

SUTRA XII

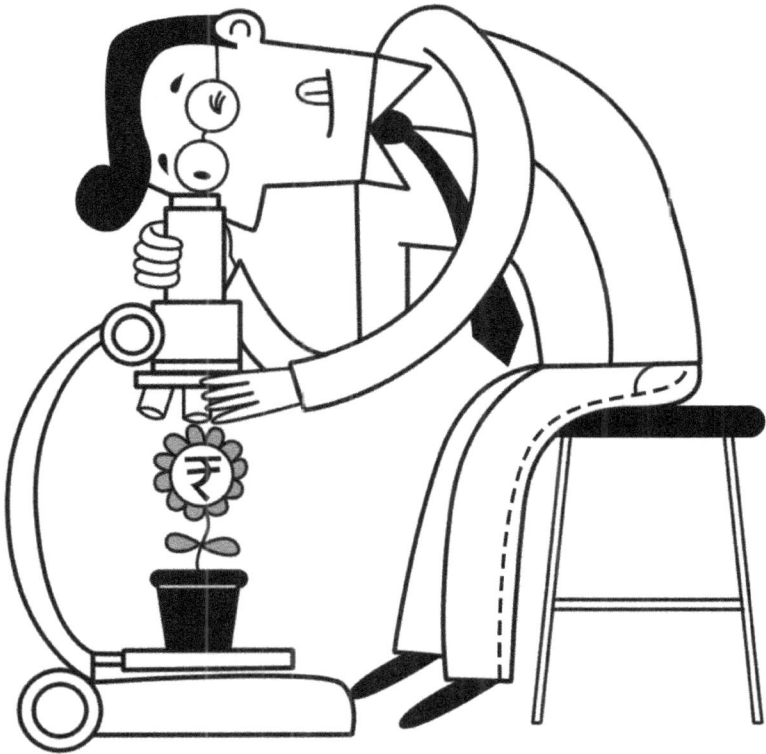

WHAT DO INVESTORS LOOK FOR BEFORE INVESTING?

> **Investing should be more like watching paint dry or watching grass grow. If you want excitement, take $800 and go to Las Vegas**
>
> – Paul Samuelson

WITH INTERNET CAME THE entrepreneur who morphed from the plodding businessman to a new age, agile, almost magical, thinker. Debt became an old-fashioned word associated with the boring, pot-bellied businessman. Equity was the new shibboleth. It was zippy, it was fashionable, it had glamour and it was the language of the maverick, disruptive, irreverent entrepreneur!

Equity brought with it a whole new investment culture. To begin with, whilst debt was associated with banks, which were government institutions, and therefore seen as highly regulated and restricting, equity came with the 'private' tag. Private, as in large finance companies in the private sector, who had the wherewithal to mobilize capital for the express purpose of purchasing stake in high potential companies,.

Although private equity as an asset class emerged in the

late 1940's, it gained currency only in the 1990's and became synonymous with Internet entrepreneurship during the 1999-2002 dotcom bubble. Equity investment heralded an industry not just of private enterprise, which was associated with huge appetite for risk, but also a corporate culture, which encouraged spotting and investing in the business ideas that defied conventional metrics.

There has been a rapid rise in equity markets fueled by investments in internet-based companies. During the dotcom bubble of the late 1990s, the value of equity markets grew exponentially, with the technology-dominated NASDAQ index rising from under 1,000 to 5,000 between 1995 and 2000.

Many say it was this over-enthusiasm with new age ideas that eventually caused the dotcom bubble to burst. In my reckoning, this may not have been such a bad thing. We tell entrepreneurs who are about to start up: FAIL EARLY, meaning to say, figure out that you are doing something wrong before you blow away too much time, effort and money. And that is exactly what happened with the private equity business. In less than a decade, they had arrived, engaged, failed and reinvented themselves.

The dotcom in late 90's and early 2000 was the flavor of the season and everyone jumped on to the bandwagon of investing in Internet startups based on their business idea, and little else. The little else was what caused the massacre. The investors got carried-away by the business ideas, because the ideas seemed so outrageous, their business model, so unbelievable, the returns, so fetching. Nothing like what they were used to before, in the manufacturing space.

They did not validate the market because there was no market to validate. They did not ponder over whether customers would gravitate towards the product simply because, up until then, the market place dynamics was such that the customer was seen as a passive consumer who neither had spine nor a mind of his own.

Phrases like 'user behavior' had not entered the language of business. So the assumption was that there is an idiot out there who has a loaded wallet, you give him what he wants and he will pull his wallet out.

But the biggest mistake they also made was they did not check the staying and building power of the entrepreneurs in whose idea they were investing. That essentially is what caused the famous dotcom bust.

The Father of Ecommerce in India

There have been entrepreneurs like K. Vaitheeswaran whose idea was so ahead of it's times that it almost seemed pre-ordained to fail. Yet, Vaitheeswaran not only stayed for fourteen years in that business, even though his co-founders quit when the going got rough, he even reinvented the model, hived off a part of it and continued to run the part that had originally drawn him to the idea and excited him the most. I'm talking about India's first ecommerce company, fabmall.com.

Vaitheeswaran got his first exposure to the Internet in the late '90's when he was working in Wipro. From the word go, he was hooked and the more he browsed, the more it occurred to him that the Internet had the potential to change the way Indians shopped (what a prophetic vision!) So he quit a high paying job at Wipro to start Fabmall in Bangalore with his own savings.

Before he quit, he had a talk with his wife Radhika who ran a placement company. Radhika told him to chase his dream but she said, before you do that, make sure we have a roof over our heads. So before Fabmall came into existence, they bought themselves a one-bedroom house.

Fabmall started off with hardly any fanfare. If I remember right, there were several co-founders, all from Wipro. I get goose bumps even as I write this – the sheer audacity of the team – to even conceptualize an ecommerce business at a time when Internet was absolutely new. There were hardly any users in India, there was no concept of a portal, there were no payment gateways, there was no notion of back-end mechanism for order fulfillment and most importantly, there were no logistics companies to do doorstep delivery. Sometimes I wish I could have been a fly on the wall and had eavesdropped on the team even as they ideated. For the life of me, I can't wrap my head around the fact that they actually managed to get the product off the ground!

Don't forget, there was no market place model then. So Fabmall had to purchase all the products that they made available on their portal. The inevitable double whammy happened. They could not drive traffic to the portal for several reasons. The Internet penetration was abysmal. The customers were not used to shopping unseen. The only other model that existed which was similar to this was catalogue shopping which was a big disaster anyway. And credit card usage itself was confined to a handful of shoppers.

In other words, everything that could go wrong went wrong. Sometimes I wonder if Vaitheeswaran and team had even factored in all these showstoppers at all. Maybe like typical entrepreneurs, they were so excited with their product that they did not stop to think of all the negative what if scenarios, the biggest one being, what if there is no customer!

If, not factoring absence of infrastructure and user acceptance was the first big mistake, the second, and much bigger one, was made as a knee-jerk response to fix the first. Since inventory had piled up, the team decided to open physical stores called Fabmall and that perhaps was the trigger to the downward spiral.

The stores were hugely capital intensive as it involved expensive real estate, manpower, licenses and infrastructure costs. As more stores opened, the costs escalated and it was a while before the team realized that in retail business, there were no economies of scale!

In the meantime, although the company had raised some capital, the burn rate was so high that very soon they ran out of money. The two co-founders and employees quit and Vaitheeswaran bravely held on to the sinking ship.

When the Aditya Birla group was shopping for retail outlets in 2006, Vaitheeswaran quickly hived off the physical stores, sold them to the Birlas who renamed Fabmall as More. The ecommerce part of the business was renamed indiaplaza.com and Vaitheeswaran was all set for his second innings with his first love!

Then, he ran out of money. For a company that had raised just Rs 40 crores in its 14 years of existence, this was not easy. And there were no takers. Vaitheeswaran told the Indiaplaza pioneering story to anyone who cared to listen but by then, the investors only heard resounding words like Flipkart and Snapdeal. Finally, the curtain came down on 12ᵗʰAugust, 2013. That day, Vaitheeswaran may have gone home a disenchanted man but for me, ecommerce will always be synonymous with Vaitheeswaran.

> Indiaplaza raised Rs 25 crores from Kalaari Capital in 2011. But by mid-2012 Vaitheeswaran was back in the market, looking for another Rs 25 crores.

Why did the investors not buy into the Indiaplaza story? By 2012, ecommerce in India was the poster boy of Internet industry. As a pioneer, this company should have been the cock of the walk. It is not as if the company had a weak topline. It had a gross merchandise value (GMV) of Rs 38 crores, which may not have stood well in comparison with Flipkart or Amazon, but it wasn't a number that could be easily dismissed either.

The company was making losses but then, investment decision in Internet companies has never been driven by profit, right? If that was the case, none of the ecommerce companies could have raised any capital at all! The company had a small team of about 30 people, it was present in a few select categories like books and electronics and it was looking to add more. Yet, the story did not excite the investors.

My reading of the situation is this: Although Vaitheeswaran invested in technology to create both a robust back end and user interface, it wasn't enough. He was a technocrat, so I refuse to believe that he did not understand technology. Perhaps he chose to be conservative in his spend, as money was tight? The result was that the customer experience was rather heavy-footed and lugubrious. I can say this, having been a customer myself.

When I bought some books, there was no delivery for over a month. When I called customer care, I was told they had been delivered, when I protested that I had not received the books, I was curtly told that 'that is not their problem'. Their books showed that the books were delivered and that was it. I pleaded, threatened, yelled, all to no avail. Three days later, a courier appeared mysteriously and delivered my books!

The story didn't end here. Since I had ordered through an educational institution, they were supposed to collect the payment after delivery. Neither did they send me the invoice nor did they come to collect payment, despite repeated phone calls. Finally based on the order summary, I simply mailed them the check.

Maybe the vendors had stopped their supplies, as their dues were not cleared; maybe the employees had lost interest as their salaries were delayed. Whatever the reason, even before the company got caught up in the vicious cycle of no money-no-customer experience, the downward spiral had already begun. I always say this; you need to raise capital when you don't need it desperately. Maybe Indiaplaza should have raised money much earlier. Maybe it should have raised more money at the time it did, so that, that money could have been invested in designing a compelling customer experience.

One more reason for not being able to excite the investors was that there was no great team. Vaitheeswaran was the only one who had stayed on from the original team of co-founders. The team he had hired when he started Fabmall had quit a long time ago. When he re-invented the business as Indiaplaza, he put together a small, functional team that neither demonstrated any great passion for their product nor competence that went beyond the requirement of role. The only magical thinker, it seemed, was Vaitheeswaran, and rarely do investors bet on solo players.

Another reason for Indiaplaza's inability to raise money may well have been Vaitheeswaran himself. He was almost a generation older when compared to the founders of other successful companies and I don't mean just the ecommerce companies. He was also a typical conservative Tamil Brahmin, who would not even talk big numbers in expenses, much less actually spend them.

Vaitheeswaran had no mojo. He was not flamboyant, he didn't have it in him to sell igloos to Eskimos, and he didn't demonstrate a burning desire to build a unicorn. I also think that he did not know to sing the song that would resonate with the investor. He was an old-fashioned engineer who tried to build a business around haute couture!

All of it boils down to one simple truth. Vaitheeswaran was a brilliant ideator but a poor implementer. The tragedy is that he may not even have known that. I don't know whether the investors realized this but the fact that they chose not to invest tells me that they probably did.

So what can we deduce from Vaitheeswaran's story with respect to what investors look for before investing? Let's review some of them:

Low cost of customer acquisition

An idea may be intrinsically brilliant but for it to be successful, it may take a lot of time, effort and money as it may involve radically changing user behavior. We have seen this in the Indiaplaza story.

Internet shopping may have been a brilliant idea in retail, but its success depended on changing the way customers viewed shopping. For instance, in smaller towns, shopping is considered a source of family entertainment. People like touchy-feely shopping. And across all age groups, shopping is more of a social engagement. And here was Indiaplaza rewriting these rules of user behavior by saying that you can shop from the confines of your home, in isolation, without either touching the product or even trying it.

And to top it all, you can do all of this by using something called the Internet and against your credit card, your unwillingness be damned!

Imagine what a Herculean task it was to bring about change of this magnitude, and on so many fronts. Imagine the cost of bringing about this change and then acquiring customers!

Investors are very wary of companies that have a high cost of customer acquisition. This would mean that their returns would be smaller, their exit would be delayed and a lot more capital may be required to hit the growth trajectory.

Winning team

Post the dotcom bust, investors have been giving less primacy to the business idea and more to the team backing the idea. The stand they take now is – and they have obviously learnt this the hard way – a great idea may fall by the wayside if the team is mediocre; conversely, a mediocre idea may be vested with greatness if the team is brilliant.

The investors prefer to invest in teams where there are multiple co-founders, who bring complementary skill-sets to the table. It is of little use if there are four co-founders and all of them are coders. Whilst it is way too ideal to expect that the four co-founders are from technology, marketing, HR and finance backgrounds, respectively. A balanced team is one where the founding team has a rounded exposure to all aspects of building the business.

A husband-and-wife founding team is not really the investors' favorite for obvious reasons. The concerns are manifold. Will they maintain professionalism in the work – space? Will they be able to compartmentalize their home from work and vice versa? In the event of a relationship breakdown, will they have the maturity to not let it affect the business?

Overall, in the founding team, the investors look for a combination of domain knowledge, skill in mobilizing and managing resources and the right attitude to grow the company ambitiously but fairly.

It goes without saying that investors are interested only in full-time entrepreneurs, who have skin in the game.

Rarely do the investors want to be the prime-movers in a domain

Interestingly, investors have a serious herd mentality. They invest in domains, which are the flavor of the season. Rarely do investors fund a business, which is a prime mover in its industry. Typically the idea should be tried and tested, there should be a couple of poster boys in that space and there should be plenty of buzz around the business. Only then will the investor talk term sheet.

Scale, scale and scale

This is a non-negotiable mantra with the investors. The business idea should be scalable across geographies, across customer segments and across product lines. Gone are the days when scale happened over a generation. The investors' window to make money and exit is three, maximum five, years and the business should lend itself to scaling up and yielding within that time frame. They tend to gravitate towards entrepreneurs who are unreasonable, impatient and aggressive.

Robust innovation pipeline

Single product, single market and single segment companies don't excite investors at all. One of their all-time favorites is a Gantt chart that shows, over the next three years, a phased plan for new products, new features, new customers, and simply new ways of doing things. The valuation typically is a multiplier of this innovation pipeline.

Capability to absorb capital like a sponge

This is related to scale. In your first round of fund-raising, you would have earmarked capital for growth. Typically you may have identified technology, geography, customer acquisition, and branding and talent management as your areas of capital deployment. Typically, you would have linked this capital deployment to X percentage of top-line growth. If it happens as planned, then very soon you will be ready for your next round of funding. That is very important for the investor as without this growth, your business will not be able to absorb capital and if it cannot absorb capital, the investor cannot exit.

Big return on investment and timely exit

This is the most obvious one. The investor is in the business of investing to make money, for his stakeholders. So right at the time of investing, he spells it out clearly, the return he expects, the time frame in which he expects the return and when he plans to exit as an investor from the company. Let's look at the investment – and – highly successful exit-track record of Chryscapital, the $2.5 billion, NewDelhi-based private equity major.

> Chryscap went bullish on the Pharmaceutical sector a few years ago, which paid off rich dividends. In 2014, Chryscap exited IntasPharma by selling its stake to Temasek for $160 million, making over 20-fold return. In early 2015, Chryscap had partially exited Torrent Pharma for around Rs 200 crore, and in the process had netted over three times return in less than 18 months. In November 2015, Chryscap exited Mankind Pharma with over 13 times return. It had invested $21 million for an 11 % stake and it sold for $200 million. In the last one year alone, Chryscap has netted over $400 million from its Pharma exits.

Exit is as important to the investor as return. The investor can exit in three ways:

❖ In the first scenario, your business has grown as per plan or even better and at the end of the three-year period, you are ready to raise more capital. This is the investor's opportunity to exit by selling his stake at market valuation to the new investor

❖ The second scenario is, if you, the entrepreneur, decide to buy out the investor's stake

❖   The third scenario is if you decide to go to the stock market
    by doing an IPO

The second scenario rarely happens. For the third to happen,
it takes at least 8 to 10 years. Therefore the first is the only feasible
and likely exit option for the investor.

Summary

Equity capital is also known as risk capital. All the risk is the
investors'. So the investors typically have some tick boxes, which
they use to evaluate the entrepreneur and his business idea.
Broadly, they validate the idea by subjecting it to the FSP test. Is
the idea feasible, scalable and profitable? Then they validate the
credentials of the entrepreneur in terms of his knowledge, skill and
attitude. Both the entrepreneur and his idea have to fare well in
this evaluation, for the investor to take the conversation forward.

TAKEAWAYS

- Investors base their decisions on tangible metrics
- The metrics are related to the execution capability of the
  entrepreneur, the implementability of the idea and the
  quick return and exit it would give the investor
- Since equity investments are risk based, the investors try to
  manage the risks by operating in their comfort zone

SUTRA XIII

CHOOSING YOUR INVESTOR

> " Games are won by players who focus
> on the playing field, not by those whose
> eyes are glued to the scoreboard. "
>
> – Warren Buffett

SOMETIMES I THINK entrepreneurship has captured the imagination of Indians in a big way, in the last five years, thanks to the high glamour quotient of being 'funded by venture capitalists'. I have been on several shows about startups on TV, as a juror, and I have always found it interesting that when I meet the participants, the first thing they tell me about their business is that they have been funded. Somehow that seems to be the biggest validation of their success as an entrepreneur! I rarely hear them rave about their customer engagement, the excitement of their teams in building and delivering a disruptive product, or the cofounders' vision. It is always about how they have just been funded.

Why does the investor so dominate the psyche of the entrepreneur? Yes, he brings the oxygen that juices up his start-up engine to run the race, but I think, apart from the purely economic reason, it is also because of the related buzz words that come with him. Words like unicorn, valuation (which, going by the current market, the more obscene, the better), capital(in several million dollars which in themselves seem mind numbing, but when translated to crores simply knock you out), consortium of investors (the more the number of investors, the more investible you appear to be), share subscription agreement (the document that details how many shares you have agreed to sell to the investor and at what price), etc. All of them have a magical quality about them because somehow they make you, the entrepreneur feel that you have risen above the ordinary, that you have joined the big leagues.

Irrespective of your age, if something makes you feel so chuffed, it can't be a bad thing. But it could go bad if you don't pay attention to one important detail. Just the way you draw up a job description for your employees before you hire them, or have a wish list of what you want from your spouse, you need to articulate what you want from your investor and then choose the one who fits the bill.

The problem is, if you were to ask entrepreneurs what they want from their investors, the answer will be an incredulous look that says: duh, what I want is money! This is where the mismatch begins and you can read the epitaph of that relationship even before it begins.

Yes, you want money, but money in itself is useless if your investor does not participate in the strategic growth of your business, which means along with money, he should bring his knowledge, skill, attitude, commitment and network to the table.

Knowledge

An investor who has little knowledge of your domain and therefore does not understand the dynamics of the marketplace in which you operate would be a disaster. If he is just a passive investor and keeps himself away from your day-to-day business, the biggest upside is that he is not interfering in your business but the biggest downside is that your business is deprived of his perspective and insights.

Skill

Apart from the business skill or the organizational skill, it will be hugely beneficial if your investor has the skill of investing in start-ups. This is a highly under-rated skill. In all my conversations with investors, I have realized that most of them treat start-ups as 'mini large organizations'. So they assume that the lessons they have learnt from working and investing in large organizations have to be simply migrated to the start-ups, although in a miniature fashion.

Nothing could be farther from truth. A start-up is a person in its own right. It is not a baby that is waiting to grow up!! It is not an entity way down below the organization totem pole. So if you were to apply the principles of management that are relevant for a large organization, to a start-up, you would be doing tremendous disservice to the latter. Every organization has to 'act its age'. Yes, a large organization is expected to be nimble-footed like a start-up, but it can't make the mistakes a start-up does. Similarly, a start-up is expected to behave with maturity when it comes to expending its resources but that does not mean it has, at its disposal, an over-sized war chest!

Attitude

What is attitude? Interestingly, Social Psychology defines it as a combination of cognition and conation. The dictionary definition of cognition is 'the act or process of knowing, perceiving'. Knowing what? If you are in the midst of traffic and you hear an ambulance siren just behind you, you 'know' the following, instantly. An ambulance means:

❖ A health emergency

❖ You are expected to make way for the ambulance

❖ Not only you, all others in the traffic are expected to make way

❖ That is the only time you are not irritated with someone honking

Knowing this, everyone in the traffic does the impossible, which is, somehow create the right of passage for the ambulance.

This is cognition. What is conation?

Going with the same example, why do we make way for the ambulance? It is not enough that we know. All of us know that when there is a red light at the traffic signal, we are expected to stop. But many of us don't, even knowing that we are supposed to. So how come we make way for the ambulance without even an argument?

The answer lies in conation, which refers to our desire to be recognized as 'one of the others'. Can you imagine being singled out in the traffic as someone who did not make way for the ambulance? Also in this context I think besides the desire of not wanting to be singled out, there is also the desire that one day, god forbid, if you are in the ambulance, everyone in the traffic will make way for you. So your good attitude in traffic of co-operating with the ambulance has as much to do with your knowledge that there is someone who needs to get to the hospital immediately as your desire that some day, if you are ever in the ambulance, the traffic will make way for you. This is conation. Together, this makes your attitude one of a good, evolved, responsible citizen's.

When you are choosing your investor, a good attitude is hugely important on the part of both of you. For your investor, good attitude represents a number of things. It means that when you met him the first time, no alarm bells rang in your head. It means he made you fell comfortable, which translates to:

❖ He listened to you (I have heard stories of how an investor was on his Whatsapp right through the entire pitch by an entrepreneur);

❖ He engaged in a conversation with you (not just criticized you, or loftily told you that you are looking at all the wrong things);

❖ He paid attention to you as if those few moments with you were important in his life too (not like he was doing a favor to you or was bored but suffered you through).

You never realize the importance of all of this because you are too self-obsessed with 'making an impression' on him. I have heard from entrepreneurs who had a rough journey with their investors that they had a 'bad feeling' about the guy, the first time they met him, but when he took his checkbook out, they forgot about it! Not only should you not forget, you should learn to cross check with your gut feel.

These first impressions translate to a number of necessary adjectives. Like, trust, faith, comfort. If you don't feel you can trust him, or if you feel he has no faith in your capability to implement the business plan or if you are not comfortable because you don't think you both are on the same page in terms of the growth vision for your company, you should not take the conversation forward.

Commitment

Another under-rated metric while choosing an investor is an assessment of how committed he is to commitment! This is not just about having belief in your idea or having faith in your ability to deliver. Let us accept the fact that he may have no commonality with you or your disruptive business plan. His only interest may be in using your grand vision to maximize his return. That is his dharma. Within this framework, is he committed to making sure that you do everything by the book – whether it is building better products to enrich customer experience or building a high performance culture within the organization? Or is his interest governed only by deploying funds in building your brand visibility so that he gets a profitable and timely exit? You need to figure this one out before you sign the term sheet.

Network

Like I said right at the beginning, you need the investor to bring to the table, more than just money. He needs to be able to open doors for you and this is almost as important as the money that he brings. Irrespective of the stage of the start-up, network is one thing that never goes out of fashion, or become unimportant. An investor's network may span a wide array of connections which may be in:

- ❖ Your domain, which will help you build better products;
- ❖ Your catchment area, which will enrich your portfolio of customers;
- ❖ Bringing on board the next set of investors;
- ❖ Putting together a robust, credible Advisory Board, and
- ❖ Being able to connect you with excellent mentors.

Let's look at how Alibaba not only invested in Paytm but also played a strategic role. The partnership has resulted not just in the phenomenal growth of the company but also in the way it gave courage and conviction to its founder, Vijay Shekar Sharma, to think big.

Ant Financial, which is the investing arm of Alibaba, took a 40% stake in Paytm in early 2015 for Rs 4700 crore. But it didn't just stop with bringing capital to the table. The first area that Jack Ma, the founder of Alibaba focused on was de-risking payments.

Out of 2.5 million transactions that took place on Paytm every day, about 0.12% of them were fraudulent. Whilst the percentage in itself seemed very small, its impact on profitability and growth of the company was huge. Earlier Paytm had 5 engineers working in risk. Jack Ma brought in 15 high profile engineers from China to work out of Paytm's Noida office so that the percentage could be reduced to an internationally acceptable level of 0.003%. According to Sharma, Alibaba made them 'think like a big company and not a start-up'.

Alibaba is working with Paytm closely in two areas – technology and business. According to Sharma, "our outlook of business execution has changed now. Earlier I was bothered about getting 100 million or 500 million users. Now it's the potential of new businesses that we can do, with this large user base."

Alibaba is an expert at handling scale and the partnership is helping Paytm build not only the largest payment cloud in the country but also expand its catchment area. Suddenly the time to go to market has shrunk as Alibaba puts its huge ecommerce machinery behind Paytm. Consequently, Vijay Shekar Sharma is no longer afraid of scale!

At different stages in the life of your start-up, it needs different kinds of investors. At the seed fund stage, it needs an investor who can also help with prototyping and customer discovery.

With a Series A investor, the requirement is that he helps in putting processes and systems in place, building a vibrant innovation pipeline, hiring the right talent at the right price, defining the growth strategy (organic or inorganic, if it is inorganic, identifying companies that can be acquired, their valuation, documentation and integration), expanding the market footprint and making a high-decibel noise for brand building.

As you can see, an investor should not be expected to just bring money!

Earlier in this chapter I had said, both you and the investor should have the right attitude. The scenario up until as late as a year ago, was that the investor never talked about bad entrepreneurs and entrepreneurs never talked about bad investors. If an entrepreneur bribed his customer, siphoned off money, engaged in sexual harassment of his team, the investor maintained stoic silence as long as this behavior did not affect revenues and profits and when it did affect negatively, he quietly walked away into the sunset and wrote it off his books.

Similarly when investors engaged in chicanery, like poaching, stealing of business plans, backing off from investing after committing, changing terms of investment midway through the engagement and the like, the entrepreneur simply blamed it on his luck of the draw and quietly retreated to lick his wounds.

But thanks to the spat between Rahul Yadav, former Co-founder and CEO of Housing.com and Shailendra Singh of Sequoia capital, India, both investors and entrepreneurs have acquired a new voice– that of social media. Given its power of reach and stridency of its tone, it has made both parties aware that each needs to be like 'Ceasar's wife', that is, simply above suspicion! My guess is that in the next year or so, we will see a new language of engagement emerging between investors and entrepreneurs, one that is transparent, objective, unbiased and goal-oriented.

Summary

In India, even to this day, investors choose entrepreneurs, not the other way. Investors do due diligence on entrepreneurs, the latter have no such luxury. Somewhere in 2011, in one of my monthly columns for *The Entrepreneur* magazine, I had said, and I'm quoting myself, "*I'm waiting for a time in India when entrepreneurs can be as picky and choosy about their VC's as the latter are. Right now, it's a lop-sided market, with all the dice loaded in the VC's favor. But I'm sure there will come a day when entrepreneurs will call the shots*".

True enough in April 2015, my mentee Nizam (www.eventstiger.com) drew my attention to this post on Staply's website:

Attention Investors: Staply user base grew by 3.97 percent last week! Want to learn more? We'll come to you and answer all your questions about Staply for $10,000. We'll fly to your city, tell you about product, business model, timeline, founders and answer all the questions you might have about Staply. We want to build a great company. To do that, we are working on Staply and talking to our users. We don't want to spend our time on emails, calls, and meetings, presentations that have high chances of not ending up anywhere. By purchasing this pitch [session for $10,000] you will assure us that your intentions with Staply are serious."

The brave new world is here and how!!

TAKEAWAYS

- Don't be blind-sided by the power of your investor's wallet
- Choose your investor carefully, diligently and for the right reasons; the ideological fit is as important as money
- Besides money, look for investors who bring knowledge, skill, attitude, commitment and network to the table
- Exercise your democratic right of choosing your investor

SUTRA XIV

WHAT IS CROWD SOURCING AND HOW DOES IT WORK?

> ## Platforms are the offices/factories of the future
> — Ernesto Spruyt, Mobbr.com

THIS IS A FORM of sachetized capital. This form of raising capital gained currency, thanks to the Internet, which facilitates handshake between the entrepreneur, who is in need of capital and a number of his 'supporters' who may not know him but like his idea. Quintessentially, crowdfunding is a model in which the idea is the hero and it magnetizes supporters.

Given the fact that it is supporter based, it is not surprising that the first instance of crowdfunding was in the music industry. But this was neither equity nor debt. It was simply a form of donation made by the rock group's fan base. The Internet facilitated it by making it possible to reach far and wide.

> In 1997, although Internet was still dodgy, the British rock group Marillion, raised money for its US tour through an Internet campaign from its fans worldwide.

Marillion was so captivated by this form of donation that from 2001 onwards, they raised money for all their albums by crowd sourcing.

In the post industrialization era, crowdfunding models existed but in a physical form. This, naturally, narrowed its catchment area and as a result of that, it limited its potential. There was probably no moderating platform or agency either, and by word of mouth, it connected the investor with the inventor.

The first time I heard of it and experienced it was when in 2011, my then co-founder wanted to participate in a business plan competition organized by a US based company called unreasonable.org. This was a very interesting concept. All the short-listed companies had to raise X amount of money on their platform (that is, on www.unreasonable.org) within a specific time frame, and the money so raised was used by the entrepreneur to fund the six-week boot camp in the US where he would get an opportunity to meet other entrepreneurs, mentors, investors etc. He would also be able to tweak his business plan with the help of mentors and investors. 25 companies that raised the prescribed amount, the fastest, would be invited to the US.

I think unreasonable.org embraced this model because this was one way of validating two things: one, how serious the entrepreneur was and two, how articulate he was in convincing people to contribute to taking his idea to market. This was also a wonderful way of validating how well the entrepreneur was networked because this money had to come from people in his own network. There was no way of bringing on board any stranger, as this was practically a donation.

The amount was very small (if I remember right, the first three weeks it was Rs. 500 per head and the last week you could go up to Rs. 1000 per head). There was a cap on the per capita amount raised, so it was a numbers game. You had to reach out to just about everyone one you knew to raise the requisite amount (if I remember correctly, we had to raise Rs. 120,000).

My co-founder did all the hard work of mobilizing this amount as he was keen on winning and going to the US. The travesty was that soon after we raised the money, we had a falling out and although my company, CARMa, was a winner, he did not represent CARMa but a company he floated for that purpose (and nothing came of it once he was back).

Although I had not been very closely involved in the process of fundraising on this kind of a platform, I found the concept interesting and at that time, I vaguely remember thinking that this might be the way of capital-raising in the future.

One of the other examples of crowdfunding was the model adopted by a Chennai-based micro credit company called rangde. org. Smitha and her husband Ram co-founded this company with a lot of passion and as they say on their website, "It is India's first low cost online crowdfunding platform that provides micro credit to low income entrepreneurs and students". This was a debt model in the sense that rangde returned your capital with interest, if you chose that option. It also gave you the opportunity to waive the principal and the interest amount, in which case, it would be treated as a donation.

A variant of this donation model is also a reward model wherein the entrepreneur may offer a small reward for donating the money. For example, let's say, a small Chinese take away joint raises money on a crowdfunding platform. They may offer a free meal for two as a reward.

This model works if the amount to be raised is small and there is no long-term expectation of a huge success. It also works well for artists' projects such as money for creating an installation or an album, or even an artists' boot camp. It also works well in raising capital for social ventures. The platform is good for raising either initial capital or even working capital, after going to market. By and large, it is easy to raise small amounts of money, let's say less than $10,000.

But the moment the capital raised is in millions and these millions are raised as a donation or reward model, paradoxically, the success of the venture breeds discontent amongst its investors! For example, Oculus Rift, a US based virtual reality company ran a campaign in 2012 on Kickstarter and raised $2.5 million. The supporters of the campaign felt shortchanged when the company was acquired by Facebook for $2 billion and they got no reward or benefit from this acquisition.

> "India might benefit from an existing crowd-funding ideal ingrained in its socio-cultural practices. The "chanda" collection for the community puja (festival) is pure, unadulterated crowdfunding.
>
> India's first crowd-funded film came way back in the 70's with Shyam Benegal's Manthan, which was produced by contributions from 2 milk farmers in Gujarat.
>
> Today, a number of prominent Indian filmmakers, musicians and entrepreneurs on the scene are waking up to the potential and power of crowdfunding. Some prominent examples include Onir (whose National Award winning film I AM was crowd-funded by more than 400 contributors); Kannada film Lucia and many more!"
>
> (**Source** *The Economic Times*, dated 27th May 2014)

Crowdfunding has evolved in the last couple of years as a platform for raising capital against a small equity in the company, the reason for its popularity is fairly obvious. Crowdfunding gives the small investor the opportunity to invest in early stage startups, which means at relatively much lower valuation and even before they have had the opportunity to take off. The risk is certainly higher at this stage, but since the platform allows the investor to invest small amounts (sometimes as low as $10), it is no skin off anyone's nose.

Many investors consider equity crowdfunding as the Holy Grail. Crowdfunding platforms themselves have attracted large amounts of angel and venture capital funding. Angels have invested, up until mid-2015, close to $393 million in the top 10 equity crowdfunding platforms and the VC's have invested close to $700 million in them. What makes them tick?

For one, this model is set to revolutionize the capital industry as it offers a win-win to both the buyer and the seller. From the seller's point of view (investor), it is beneficial as it offers them an alternate option for investment, besides the usual equity markets and debt instruments.

From the buyer's (entrepreneur) perspective, it is a high decibel, high reach, low cost capital-raising model and it offers huge economies of scale in terms of the entrepreneur's time, effort and money spent on raising the capital.

For another, typically the returns are higher than any other investment, especially if the investor is willing to stay invested for at least 5-7 years. It may not be as stupendously high as a Facebook (62000%) or a Dropbox (39000%) but it will certainly be very attractive.

The biggest upside of this model is that it gives the entrepreneur the opportunity to access global investors and not just those in his geography. Conversely, it gives the investors the opportunity to look beyond their hyper local catchment area, participate in the growth story and reap a rich harvest from it.

In other words, it creates a new asset class that is diversified, vibrant and robust.

If I have given the impression, up until now, that crowdfunding is a cakewalk, it is time to disabuse you of that notion! If you treat it as a strategic marketing tool (and here you are marketing not to your customers but investors who may also be your customers, but your pitch is to raise capital, not sell your product), and you do all that needs to be done to use this tool effectively, you will see success. Let us understand what are the things you need to do to ensure success of your campaign.

Evaluate whether crowdfunding is the right platform for your product

Not all products work on crowd-funding platforms. Your product has to be something that has a high emotional connect with people. If your product is an ERP software, it is highly unlikely that it will attract investors, for the simple reason there is neither a fun element in it, nor is it glamorous or interesting. On the other hand, if your product is clip-on nail art or video games, or interesting gadgets (for example, a Logitech mouse that looks like a cat), or shoes with changeable straps and heels, your chances of running a successful campaign is very high. Choose crowdfunding only if you have disruptive or high attention-seeking or curiosity-arousing products.

Choose the right platform

There are any numbers of Crowdfunding platforms both in India and across the world. Choose the one that fits the best with your ideology. For example, you may choose Kickstarter as your platform. If the platform is known largely for raising money for social ventures or projects (and it is, it does not do equity), chances are that people who gravitate towards the platform looking for potential investment opportunities are those who are interested in social ventures. In which case, no amount of campaigning from your side will draw blood.

Choose the right time

Pretty much across the world, you will not see much investor footfall during the holiday season. Choose the season correctly. Also in India, there are months such as Ashad and Pithru Paksh that are considered inauspicious and during that time, investors do not venture out. So choose a time that sees good roaring business (Diwali is a wonderful time). Typically the second and third quarters of the Financial Year, barring the bad months, are a good time for raising capital. The first quarter always tends to be slow with everyone in a wait-and-watch mode. The last quarter sees people engrossed in cleaning and wrapping the year up.

Hire a professional to create your collaterals

This is one investment you have to make, even if it means selling the shirt off your back. The collaterals may be a brochure, or a video or even a simple slideshare. Make sure that it is eyeball grabbing. Your window of opportunity to attract your investors is very limited. You should sucker-punch them the moment they start going through your campaign. No way they will go without taking their checkbook out, dude!

Articulate clearly

Let your message be clear and crisp. The message, in 60 seconds or less (video), in 300 words or less (brochure), should tell the investors very clearly, what is your product and how it will change the world. Use simple but effective words. Don't appear as if you have swallowed a dictionary!

Convey your passion intelligently

Don't blubber or load your message with too much overarching emotion! Remember this is not the prime time TV serial, which is mandated to be a tearjerker! Even if your product can eradicate AIDS from the face of the earth, don't dish out sentimental or jargonized drivel. Use your intelligence to show them your heart!

Tell your story

Nothing attracts and registers better than a story. Weave a story around your product. Tell it with feeling, with involvement, with sensitivity (I'm saying sensitivity because I once sat through a pitch where the entrepreneur was pitching for a product that was a vaginal contraceptive. He was doing fine till he decided to drive home the point. He looked at me balefully and said: "if your daughter was raped ma'am, wouldn't you be glad to know that she never steps out of the house without applying the vaginal contraceptive which remains active for 24 hours?" Not only did I want to throw up (I had a teenaged daughter at that time) but I also wanted to bash him up!

Yes, it works well when you personalize it, when you engage the investor, but you should do it with empathy and sensitivity.

Create awareness about your product much before you start the campaign

This is very important. Most entrepreneurs sign up for a three-month campaign on a platform and go home disappointed that they hardly had any response. Use all the low cost media available at your disposal to create awareness. It could be word-of-mouth, it could be your social media, it could be your network's media, it could be some entrepreneurial events at TiE, use anything, at least three months before you start your campaign on the platform. The run up to the campaign should be a huge buzz online and off line, such that you have aroused enough interest and curiosity in your network and they are actually waiting to participate in your campaign. Use your mentor's brand equity to create the buzz!

Leverage your network

Let's be realistic, your first fifty percent of money required should come from people known to you and you need to onboard them with zeal. The psychology here is very simple. If you see two eateries side by side, one is choc-a-bloc with customers and the other is empty, as someone who is hungry and looking for good food, which one will you choose? Obviously the packed one, logic being that so many people can't be wrong.

Apply the same logic here. If people come to view your campaign and find that there are no takers, they will walk away, but if they see frenetic activity and the meter is ticking like never before, they will want a piece of the action before it withers away. Creating that impression of frenetic activity is your primary responsibility and you can do this, not with strangers, but with people from your own network.

Having a mentor works wonders here as you can leverage his/her network, big time.

Don't make promises that you don't intend to keep

This is a matter of credibility and if you are not careful in your messaging or you willfully convey a lie, or hide the truth, it could damage you forever. I remember a couple of years ago a youngster started a campaign on one of the Crowdfunding platforms for a homemade antidote to the Ebola virus. He raised almost $50000 before it came to the attention of someone form a government agency in the US, which dealt with such deadly viruses. Investigation revealed that the antidote was a simple placebo and had none of the properties he had claimed. When he was asked why he ran the scam, his answer was he planned to use the money he raised on the platform to start work on a possible antidote!

Be realistic about how much money you want to raise

According to Kickstarter, less than 2% of the successful campaigns raised more than $100,000 in 2014. Close to 73% of the successful campaigns raised around $10,000. The psychology of "if I ask for more, I will get something at least", doesn't work here. Be realistic as to how much you need, and why. Just as you would do in a regular pitch to the investor; your pitch on the platform should clearly enunciate, along with what your product is, and its value proposition, how much money you need and how you plan to use it. Clearly show how this money will fund growth and not just some revenue expenses.

Be prepared to be available all the time during the campaign

Don't assume that now that you have listed on a platform, you are off the hook. Now is the time to be available, monitoring, taking calls or replying to emails if someone reaches out to you, clarifying, cajoling, even coercing gently. Come across as someone who has the right attitude. Unnecessary aggression or passivity will be detrimental to your efforts. The best run campaigns are those that allow the investor to first fall in love with the entrepreneur and then his product. It is a full-time job and it requires you to put your best foot forward.

The top 10 global crowdfunding sites:

1. **AngelList** is a US website for raising equity or debt investments for startups. Only accredited investors can invest at the time of writing.

2. **Early Shares** is an Equity Crowd-Funding Platform Crowdfunding American Small Businesses.

3. **Crowdcube** is an equity-based UK crowd-funding platform.

4. **Fundable** is a crowd-funding platform that offers both rewards-based and equity-based campaigns for small businesses.

5. **Seedrs** is an equity crowd-funding platform for discovering and investing in seed-stage startups, based in the United Kingdom but open to investors and entrepreneurs throughout Europe.

6. **CircleUp** is an equity-based crowd-funding site based in San Francisco.

7. **Crowdfunder** is a global social network for equity and contribution crowdfunding for small businesses, startups and social enterprises.

8. **WeFunder.com** "We help everyone invest in startups. It's like Kickstarter, but with equity."

9. **Equity Net** was launched in 2005 and "is the original and only patented crowdfunding platform. It is used by thousands of entrepreneurs, investors, government entities, business incubators, and other members of the entrepreneurial community to plan, analyze, and capitalize privately-held businesses."

10. **RockThePost** is an equity crowdfunding platform that connects high quality entrepreneurs with accredited investors interested to invest in exciting new start-up companies.

Source: Salvador Briggman's undated article on Crowd Crux

Indiegogo and Kickstarter have not officially moved into the equity crowdfunding space at the time of writing, but it has long been speculated that they will. This is also true of RocketHub.

Strangely enough, hardly any noteworthy sites in India are equity crowdfunding platforms. There are a number of donations or rewards based platforms such as Wishberry, Catapoolt, Indiegogo, Ketto, Bitgiving and the like.

Equity platforms

However, there are a few startups, which have ventured into the area of exchange-like platform for equity funding. For example, GREX Alternative Investments Market helps startups raise capital against equity from multiple investors who are on their platform. The others in this category are LetsVenture, Termsheet, and Equity Crest.

However they are different from Crowdfunding platforms in a few ways:

❖ They charge a commission from the company wanting to raise capital

❖ In crowdfunding platforms, since they are donations-based, the investors do not expect any return. But on these platforms, investors expect quick and huge returns

❖ On these platforms, number of investors would be limited unlike in regular Crowdfunding platforms where since the ticket size is small, the number of investors could run to thousands

❖ The capital on these platforms is raised against equity. The founding team of the startup, which intends to raise capital, has to divest their equity holding in favor of the investors

❖ All of them claim that they do due diligence of both investors and startups. LetsVenture for instance, says that the start-ups are curated before showcasing them on their platform LetsVenture, which is a Bangalore-based equity platform says on its website that it has funded, as on early 2016, 60 startups and raised $18 million

❖ Many of these platforms have started syndicates to induct new investors and are paid by the investment gains for their services

❖ The amounts raised on this platform could range anywhere from Rs 1–6 crores.

(Source for equity platforms: *The Economic Times* dated 14th January 2016)

The exit for investors on these platforms typically is when they divest in favor of the promoters or new investors. There is also a proposal to link this to the secondary market by allowing platforms like GREX to set up the secondary exchange too. SEBI(Securities and Exchange Board of India)has appointed a committee under Narayan Murthy to examine the implications, frame rules, recommend new frameworks and also suggest changes that need to be made in the law.

Summary

Crowdfunding is a newly emerging tool that has seen success in raising small amounts more for projects than products.

There is no doubt that crowdfunding as an important alternative capital source for startups, is here to stay. At this point in time, crowdfunding in India is largely donations based and seems to be raising money for social causes, predominantly.

I'm also sure in the next few years we will see equity-based platforms mushrooming, as this is that one key stake-holder missing in the Indian entrepreneurial habitat today.

I'm equally sure that before this happens, the regulatory framework has to be put in place by the government. Equity is complex both in terms of valuation as well as documentation. It is very important that SEBI (lays down the rules clearly on all the modalities of managing this kind of capital raised against equity.

TAKEAWAYS

- Choose this mode of fundraising wisely, it should be a decision led by strategy and not by the buzz
- There are a number of Indian platforms for crowdfunding, but most of them are donations or rewards based. Equity based Crowdfunding is yet to gain currency in India
- Keep in mind all the dos and don'ts to ensure the success of your campaign
- Regulatory framework for equity based crowdfunding in India is yet to be formulated

SUTRA XV

WHEN IS THE RIGHT TIME TO BE AN ENTREPRENEUR WHEN YOU ARE A WOMAN?

> **A bell is just a cup, until it is struck**
>
> – Album from the rock group, Wire.

IN INDIA, THERE IS never a right time for a woman to be an entrepreneur. Tragic and brutal as it sounds, it is the truth. Let's say you are in your final semester of engineering and you have this brilliant idea for a business. You go to your dad and share it with him. Chances are that he will say, it is all very well, beta, but first get married and then you start the business. If you start one now, and the man is not from around where we are, and you will have to move to wherever he is, what will happen to the business?

So you park the idea on the back burner till you get married. Even before the mehendi has dried on your hands, you go to your husband and share the idea with him. He is hugely excited, he says, but honey, let's first have a baby, then you can start the business. So your park the idea on the back burner till your first child arrives. Five years go by and now your child has started school. You go back to your husband with the idea. He displays the same enthusiasm as before, but says, sweetheart, let's have the second baby, with that our family will be complete. Then you can start the business.

So you park the idea for the third time on the back burner till your second child starts school. By which time, five more years have gone by.

All in all, you have missed out over a decade. By now, others have hijacked your business idea and you are happy that they have made a success of it because it validates that your idea was bankable. You are also sad that it wasn't you who went laughing to the bank.

But this time you don't go back to your husband with any idea. You are beginning to feel desolate that you have been out of circulation for over a decade now, everything in the ecosystem has changed, between changing nappies and managing your home, you have not kept yourself abreast of business practices, technology and the economy at large.

So you really don't have it in you any more to become an entrepreneur. If the desire is very strong, you may decide to do something on a small scale, like bake chocolates and sell them amongst your own family and friends. But you no longer think you can think big.

So what are the options for women like you? A few years ago, I offered a one year course for women to up-skill them in entrepreneurship. It was meant to be an online course with a week, each quarter, of meeting face to face. More than a hundred women applied for the course, much to my delight. But there was a huge surprise in store for me when I interviewed the women.

It emerged that there were three distinct categories of women interested in the course and each category had its own agenda. What was common to them was that they were all engineers, had worked for a couple of years in corporates before getting married, had worked for a couple of years more after marriage and had taken a decade long sabbatical to have kids.

In the first category, the women said they were not keen on becoming entrepreneurs but wanted to get back to a mid-management corporate career.

In the second, the women wanted to be entrepreneurs but not the mom-and-pop store variety. They wanted to be up-skilled to start a large-scale enterprise. It was interesting that many of them said they wanted to start a Google or an Amazon!

The third category was a complete surprise. The women said that they were married to high profile corporate honchos and were neither interested in pursuing a corporate career nor did they want to become entrepreneurs. They said they wanted to be brought up to speed in terms of whatever was happening in the business world so that at office parties, they could participate in the conversation with their husband's colleagues, intelligently and confidently and not get stuck with other women, discussing babies and nannies!

Unfortunately, I have not had the bandwidth to offer this course again and I really hope some educational institution or corporate would take it upon itself to do so. Because not only is there a huge market, but it is also the need of the hour.

Let's assume that some women, despite the odds, actually do become entrepreneurs when the idea grabs their imagination. I have found it fascinating to observe their behavior. Even here, I have seen three categories.

The first one is a girl straight out of an engineering or business school, full of beans, cheered on by friends, encouraged by her favorite professor, to start a business. It is highly likely that her idea may be incubated on the college campus and she becomes the poster girl for that batch – the girl who sat out of placements to build a business.

The second category is of women who take a decade long sabbatical from their corporate careers to bear the mandatory two kids and a white picket existence and then struggle to make a business out of their hobbies – baking cakes or making *papier mâché* lamps, or running a day care center.

The third category is of those women who take no break in their corporate careers, work in large IT MNC's in 'the bay area', and come back to India either because 'the girls are growing up' or because 'my parents are growing old'. Along with their husbands or friends or former colleagues, they start a business, mostly in the Internet space.

In all the three cases, the first round of investment is from father, husband and own savings respectively. Let us say all three go to market successfully and are convinced that they can scale the business. And in order to do so, they need serious funding. So they approach venture capitalists.

How do VC's treat this overture?

In the first category, the VC's will be somewhat indulgent. They may like her business idea and may even think it has potential but they will not risk investing in it. The questions that weigh against her are:

❖ What happens when she gets married? This is a very loaded question with multiple layers. Her getting married could mean moving to another place. It could mean that the husband does not like the idea of his wife running a business, or expects her to join an MNC and bring home beaucoup bucks, instead of wasting time with a yet-to-make-money startup. It could mean: how will she manage time between being newly married, especially in India where you don't just marry the guy but his whole family? Or it could mean, what happens if she gets pregnant on her honeymoon? How will she manage the rigor of a first pregnancy with that of an equally demanding startup?

❖ What happens if she gets bored with the idea (women apparently get bored more quickly than men)? This one is layered too. She may get bored simply because she is fickle. Or she may get bored because she is not seeing the magic numbers she expected. Or she may get bored because husband is not as generous as dad when it comes to shopping money! Or worse, she hardly has any time now to enjoy the romance of a new coupling.

❖ What happens if marriage does not turn out to be the fairy tale that it was touted to be? Will she be able to run the business when she's on an emotional roller coaster, in a soured marriage? Will her startup be the first casualty both because she is not 'with it' emotionally and because she needs financial security now, so taking up a job makes better economic sense?

Interestingly, all the reasons for not investing are to do with her being a woman and nothing to do with her business idea! So the VC's may actually suggest that she get a couple of good male co-founders to offset the churn created by her gender!

In the second category, the rejection is point blank and idea related, not so much gender related. The VC's will tell her that her business idea is not feasible to scale, and if scaled not profitable enough! Why? Because she is messing around with a hobby and pretending to build a business around it.

In the third category, the woman entrepreneur's behavior becomes the showstopper. She creates an excellent pitch and makes a kickass presentation to the VC, she is extremely knowledgeable about her domain, she knows who her customer is and she has all her resource requirement pat, down to the last penny, for the next three years.

The several rounds of meetings go extremely well and on the day the term sheet has to be discussed she develops cold feet and insists on bringing a husband or a male friend to the table. Why? Because she thinks she will be short-changed in the negotiation because she is a woman! That is when the VC's develop cold feet and the deal is off the table.

> Moral of the story? Entrepreneur first, woman second! There are a few women who have beaten these odds, not just by having faith and conviction in their business idea but also by articulating it in no uncertain terms. So at the deal table what the VC sees is not a woman but a consummate entrepreneur!

Richa Kar, the co-founder of the online lingerie store, Zivame, is an excellent illustration of this.

Richa says her challenge was not so much with her gender as with her product. Since lingerie is not something people talk about openly, it was hugely challenging to get her customers to open up about the problems they faced in buying lingerie, whether it was in terms of the right fit, or variety or simply the whole experience of buying across the counter in a retail store.

Even now, she says, customers who buy online from her insist that the lingerie be packed in a small bag, and have no visible marking on it that indicates what is inside the package so that they can take delivery of an anonymous package at their office, shove it inside their handbags and carry it home, as innocuously as possible. Even her family members, although supported her entrepreneurial foray, were very reluctant to talk of her product and when people asked them about what Richa was doing, they would simply say, 'she's in retail'!

As far as the investors were concerned, Richa raised money from IndoUS Venture Partners (IVUP) fairly early. IUVP's founder Vani Kola must have been impressed with Richa's domain knowledge. After her MBA, Richa worked at Spencer's Retail and at SAP as retail consultant. It was during her stint at SAP that she had the opportunity of working with the mega brand, Victoria's Secret and this led her to research the lingerie market in India and discover the opportunity for Zivame.

So when she pitched to investors, Richa Kar came across as a knowledgeable and confident entrepreneur who had done enough homework to know what she was talking about. Her gender became irrelevant.

In the last five years, there has been a lot of agenda around diversity and inclusiveness that technology companies have focused on. There is a lot of noise in the media that there are more women in technology than before at all levels of the organization. So I was shocked to learn that IBM decided to re-launch an initiative called #HackAHairdryer on 6th December 2015 to excite women into embracing science and technology. The whole context of the initiative as well as the initiative itself is in such bad taste that there was a huge backlash on social media. The context is this.

On 6th December 1989, some extremists gunned down women engineering students in Quebec, Canada, on the ground that women had no business in engineering. In a weird way, IBM decided to commemorate this event by launching this program 26 years later, by adopting a route, which smacked of sexism. It hoped to entice women into their STEM program (science, technology, engineering and mathematics) by hash-tagging it as #HackAHairdryer because it seemed, all women cared about was their hair! I'd love to see someone do an impersonation of Eliza Doolittle and call IBM 'you presumptuous insect!'

Summary

India is perhaps one of the very few countries where there is no such thing as a right time for a woman to become entrepreneur. And even if she does become one, against all odds, it almost seems as if she has to be content with 'fooling around' with a hobby-as-business and not a commercial enterprise revolving around high technology, on account of her gender! Add to this her own insecurity that she may not cut ice at the deal table and we have a scenario that compounds the problem.

TAKEAWAYS

- Know what you are up against when you are a woman and want to become an entrepreneur in India

- The worst thing in India is the family. Do not fall into the trap of doing what your dad or husband wants you to do. This is not to say rebel against either of them. But if you have an idea and you are serious about building it, you need to reason it out with your family members that it can't wait and that you will balance it out

- The best thing is also the family and the support system it offers. Put it to good use it to become an excellent entrepreneur

SUTRA XVI

HOW DO YOU PITCH TO AN INVESTOR WHEN YOU'RE A WOMAN?

> ❝ **I always did something I was a little not ready to do** ❞
>
> – Marissa Mayer

WHAT ARE THE DO'S and don'ts women entrepreneurs should be mindful of when they pitch to investors? Their biggest challenge is how they can come to the deal table as gender-neutral entrepreneurs, yet remain the quintessential women that they are. Many years ago, my British boss had this word of admonition: "When you walk into the meeting, everyone at the table should admire the woman you are. When you spearhead the discussion, they should be in awe of your intellect. When you leave the discussion, they should regard you as a consummate professional. But all this does not make you sexless. All the while, you are making them admire the beautiful woman you are. The whole package. This is an art. Practise it."

So how does one practise this art?

Dress like a woman in love with herself

Having worked with women in the corporate sector and business for 30 years, I can safely put the majority of them in three buckets. In the first is the aggressive woman, dressed in functional pantsuits, in blacks or greys, dressed to underscore her femininity, who seems to be telling the male world that "I'm every bit as good as you because I dress like you".

In the second bucket is this disorganized, dishevelled woman whose attitude is: "Dressing up is for the girlie girls, I don't care to be one and therefore, I don't care how I look and therefore I'm as good as you!"

There's a third bucket: a few women who look graceful and gorgeous without losing their sense of accomplishment. Be like them!

Prepare like you want to win the war

This preparation is on many levels. The first is with respect to your business. You should be able to rattle off what your product is, the pain point it addresses, who is your customer and how you will acquire him, details of your team, how much money you will need and where you will get it from, how much money you will make, and what is your innovation pipeline.

The second preparation is with respect to the investor you are meeting. Get to know his profile (I'm saying 'his' because most VC's are men. Also under our Constitution, he includes she!), the domains he has invested in, and his average ticket size (this typically refers to the investment band the VC operates in. It can vary from Rs. 5 - 50 crore). In today's Google age, getting this information is not hard at all.

The third aspect is your attitude. You have to go prepared for the investor meeting, knowing that:

❖ He will ask you if you are serious about your business. He would never ask this of a guy, but because you are a woman, this will be his primary concern. You have to be able to demonstrate not only that your business is scalable, feasible and profitable but also that it is not just time-pass for you, that you will give it the priority it deserves and that you will not make raising family the excuse for lackadaisical performance. This really is the deal clincher

❖ You have to clearly demonstrate that you are the dealmaker. Even if you have male co-founders with you, make it known to the investor that it is you who will decide on the terms. Don't dither when it comes to numbers

❖ You will have a presentation and refuse to talk without one. Sometimes the investor may say, no need for a presentation, let's just talk. Politely say, no thank you, we will talk, but with my presentation. This is how you will also demonstrate that you are in control of the proceedings

❖ You have to mind your body language. Don't slouch, or fiddle with your hair, your *dupatta* or your stole. Be neither aggressive in your posture nor tentative in your demeanour

❖ Switch off your hand phone. You've come prepared to walk away with the cheque not as a batty woman taking calls from her family members but as an entrepreneur whose business idea is worth investing in

❖ And if the cheque book is not forthcoming, ask him why. Don't just slink away, defeated and then tell the whole world and its mother that he did not invest in your business because you are a woman!

It's all about control

Pay as much attention to the investor as he does to you. Watch his demeanour, and observe his choice of words. If you catch him fiddling with his phone in the midst of your presentation, stop. If he asks you to continue with your presentation, say, no problem, I will wait till you finish your work on the phone. Control, my dear woman! His male ego may hurt but his investor gut will cheer for you!

Don't come apart when he says 'Aye!'

Let's say you did such a magnificent job that he writes a check. Do not say, Oh my god, I never expected it and then collapse into a tearful mess! Feign coolness. Pretend like it is an everyday occurrence. Your attitude should be one of nonchalance, a knowing, smiling look that says, good to know you are so smart, buddy!

Although in India the number of women becoming entrepreneurs is less and the number of them being funded is even lesser, it never ceases to surprise me that a small country like Indonesia which has a population of 250 million, is doing so much better in this regard. At various global conferences, I have had the amazing opportunity of interacting with some of these very enterprising women.

- ❖ Grace Tahir runs a company called Pilih Dokter, which connects patients to good quality doctors online for advice and treatment
- ❖ Nabilah Alsagof is the founder of Doku, which is a payment gateway company, much like our very own Paytm
- ❖ Diajeng Lestari runs HijUp, which is ecommerce portal promoting Muslim fashion apparels
- ❖ Cynthia Tengarra set up BerryKitchen to provide lunch boxes to corporates

The amazing thing is that before they became entrepreneurs, they all worked in large organizations, gathered experience and went about the task of building their own business in much the same manner – professional first, woman next!

Summary

My boss used to say: you don't have to lose your dimples to project your intelligence. The challenge for a woman entrepreneur is, how can she balance her femininity with her serious head for business in all her conversations with the investors, not only without one overpowering the other but most importantly, with one actually embellishing the other!

TAKEAWAYS

- Be comfortable in your skin as a woman. The comfort of being an entrepreneur will follow as naturally as breathing in and breathing out

- Go armed. With facts, knowledge, possibilities, potential. And if there is something you don't know, say so, without feeling diminished

- The meeting with the investor is a negotiation, like any other. Women excel at it as negotiation comes naturally to them. Make the most of it

SUTRA XVII

FORMING AN ADVISORY
BOARD

> ❝ It's a funny thing about life. If you refuse to accept anything but the best, you very often get it ❞
>
> – William Somerset Maugham

MOST ENTREPRENEURS DON'T pay attention to forming an Advisory Board in the early stages of their journey. They have too many things on their platter and forming one seems to be an agenda on the very distant horizon. They also assume that when their organization becomes big, people will be attracted to their company and they will want to be on their Board. Therefore, it has to be factored in much in the future.

In fact you need a board to guide you to become big, so the earlier you start constituting a Board, the better for you and your organization. Since you are bound to be a private limited company, you have the option of setting up two Boards, a Statutory Board and the Advisory Board.

Statutory Board

The Board of Directors is mandated by the Ministry of Corporate Affairs (MCA). This is a Statutory Board and MCA offers clear guidelines on its website as to what the responsibilities of the Board are and how the members should be appointed. You can find the details on this link: http://www.mca.gov.in/MinistryV2/chapter4.html.

Typically the statutory board will consist of the founders of the company. If there are multiple co-founders, all may or may not be part of the board, and the decision may be based on their equity holding. Let's say there are four co-founders, holding 25% each, in which case, all may be on the Board or only two, based on their roles and responsibilities.

Along with the co-founders, there may be one independent director appointed to the board to ensure all statutory compliance. It is good practice to have a chartered accountant (CA) as an independent director as he would be well versed with the statutes under company laws.

The constitution of the Board as well as the details of the members has to be filed with the Registrar of Companies (RoC). The members should have Director Identification Number (DIN), which is fairly easy to obtain from the MCA. If there are any changes in membership, the changes have to be duly entered in the records of the RoC.

Like I said earlier, the MCA clearly defines what the responsibilities of the statutory board are. The very first clause says: "the Board of Directors has to exercise strategic oversight over business operations while directly measuring and rewarding management's performance. Simultaneously the Board has to ensure compliance with the legal framework, integrity of financial accounting and reporting systems and credibility in the eyes of the stakeholders through proper and timely disclosures".[1] This is where the independent director plays a crucial role.

---

[1] Source: http://www.mca.gov.in/MinistryV2/chapter4.html

Advisory Board

The second board is the advisory board. This is the one you, as an entrepreneur, should constitute for strategic reasons.

This is the Board that helps you implement your vision and make your presence felt in the marketplace. It is therefore logical to draw members from cross-domains. The two big questions you may have are: how do I attract credible names and how do I remunerate them?

The answers to both these questions are fairly easy. You have to engage with them in a 'conversation of possibility', that is, show them the potential of your business. Make no bones about what a magical thinker you are. Make it seem that the BHAG [2] that you have set for yourself is within your reach; it only needs the intellectual power of members like them. Make them buy into your vision.

They will come onboard for the excitement of participating in your growth story. It is a ringside view but they have orchestrated the bout and the outcome of the bout too, with their vision. And you might just invite them to the podium to share the prize too! The advisory board is your intellectual capital. When you put it together, you need to exercise the same kind of judgment and discretion that you would for your financial capital.

Equally, you need to exercise extreme caution in how you spend it. The advisory board members are in your corner. They came onboard, excited by the conversation of possibility *that you engaged them in.* You need every bit of their intellect, domain competence, brand equity and network to convert your conversation for possibility to conversation for action.

---

[2] Big Hairy Audacious Goal, a term that was coined by James Collins and Jerry Porras in their book in 1994, entitled Built to Last, which referred to setting of goals by the organization which were visionary and had huge emotional appeal

What kind of people should be on your board?

It depends on what kind of company you have but broadly, you can look for the following metrics:

People who have been there, done that

By this I mean people who bring to the table the breadth of their experience and exposure to best practices. This experience should encompass either general management with solid experience as a strategic business unit head of a sizeable operation (at least above $ 100 million in revenue) or hardcore domain experience in an industry leader. For example, the person may have headed the emerging markets in an organization like SAP, with complete P&L responsibility for his geographical region or he may have headed product development in a niche technology company like NetApp. He may even be an industry specialist, say Telecom, and may have worked with some of the telecom majors.

Either way, you are looking at a total corporate experience of 20 plus years. Unless he is a seasoned entrepreneur who has successfully built a recognizable brand, in which case, even 10 years of intense entrepreneurial experience will be more than enough.

Look for people from cross-domains

A Board, which has its members representing different domains, is a complete Board. Bring on board people from finance, marketing, operations, technology, design and talent management. Each one in turn will bring not only knowledge from that domain but also the network. It is also useful to bring on board someone with a completely unconnected work experience. A rank outsider can sometimes make your brand a wonderful outlier!

They should have an innovation mindset

It is not enough that they have work experience. I have met many people who are on the verge of retirement from large organizations and their ability to connect the dots is so limited that it makes me wonder whether they just plodded on without learning much from their workspace. Let me explain what I mean, by borrowing from our *Vedas*.

Very early on, our socialization process teaches us to be focused. We are told that in order to execute a task with excellence we need to stay focused with single-minded purpose and devotion. What no one tells us is that just focus is not good enough because that is what makes us plodders.

You also need to be able to take in the rest of the stuff on the horizon. This is what is famously known as 'connecting the dots' in management. In other words, you need perspective which makes you see causality like never before, synchronicity like you never thought of and impact that would stagger your imagination.

In Sanskrit, focus is called 'dhyana' and perspective is called 'darshana'. In your advisory board, you don't need dhyanees; you need darshanis! If one is a darshani, innovation comes as naturally to him as breathing in and breathing out!

They should have solid personal values

It is a travesty that, in India, we expect to conform to the highest standards of morality in our personal lives but we don't mind being dodgy (we rationalize by saying, we have to be 'flexible' in the workspace!) at work. In my reckoning, there cannot be a dichotomy between the two. You can't be, for instance, completely messy at home and very organized at work!

Many of us rationalize by saying that in your work environment, you have to be less strict with values for the larger good. I have never understood what it means!

Many times I have wondered if the Enron team was born with a flawed gene or they acquired one out of greed. The members came from Ivy League schools such as Harvard. I am sure they were indoctrinated with the same set of values that clearly distinguish good from bad by their families and educational institutions. Yet, a debacle like Enron happened (Enron was a large US-based energy major company, its management team led by Jeff Skilling perpetrated huge accounting frauds which resulted not only in its collapse but also the collapse of its accounting firm, Arthur Anderson).

Was it simply that the team decided to 'do it once' and then discovered that they couldn't stop? Was it the adrenalin rush of having gotten away with it the first time? Did they think that they had 'cracked it' and were therefore invincible? Did they feel remorse when they were indicted? Did they feel remorse that they had cheated or did they feel remorse because they were caught?

So you need men of sterling character who wouldn't know the meaning of compromise, on your Board!

It helps if they have tasted failure in their professional lives

The interesting thing about failure is that it not only makes you more realistic, it also helps you appreciate the values of humility and equanimity. Yes, the entrepreneur is a magical thinker, high on adrenalin, an audacious creature and a selfish bugger. But none of this mean that he has to be in a perpetual flap, forever like the proverbial dog engaged in a futile exercise of catching its own tail and trampling on everything that comes in its way. It helps if he's the calm sort, but if he isn't, he certainly needs a Board whose members are!

This works in three ways. In the first, the board tends to be more analytical and less judgmental when things don't go the expected way.

In the second, let's say you have gone ahead with a plan, which the board was skeptical about, to begin with. When it fails, a mature board is not going to waste time crowing: we told you so! They will lend you a hand to pick yourself up, help you dust down the shock and wear-and-tear of failure and move on with life, stronger, after having learnt some valuable lessons.

In the third, right when the plan is being discussed the Board has the maturity to caution you about the possible pitfalls and the inherent failures to keep you prepared for such an eventuality.

None of this is possible if the Board members haven't tasted failure at some point in their career.

On my list of values, humility comes right at the top. The entrepreneurial habitat is full of buzz in India today and if you have raised money once, you begin to think that you are the cat's whiskers. You are young, riding the crest of success and being showcased as a poster boy for the new age entrepreneurship. It is very easy to develop an attitude of arrogance– of hubris.

This is where the humility of your Board members can set you back on track before you do damage to yourself and your company.

Look for people who still have a zest for life

I don't mean just in terms of energy, although that is very important. I mean that they come with a desire to learn, not with the attitude that they know it all and they are there to help a poor sod who is young and immature and who desperately needs their help!

Just as a good mentor is one who comes with the 'I know some, you know some, and together we will learn more' attitude, a member of your Advisory Board must have the attitude that he know some, you know some and everyone else on the board knows some. And together we will learn much more. In my experience, this attitude that together we will all learn much more comes with humility.

Look for people whose word counts

This is a loaded requisite. It means a whole lot of things. It means that they should have credibility that comes with a good track record. It means they should be recognized not just as excellent professionals but as great human beings too. It means that they know many people out there that they can open doors for you.

Look for an ideological fit

This is very important and could almost be a deal-breaker. You and your board members have to be on the same page in terms of what you want for your company. The emotional disconnect could be in many ways. You may have a huge risk appetite, which may spur you to do things that are seen by the board as premature, unnecessarily risky and needlessly contrarian, moves. On the other hand, the board may want you to step on the accelerator and you may feel that neither you nor your company is ready for it yet.

These are what I call housekeeping disconnects and these can be easily sorted out with open communication. The ideological disconnect that I am referring to is where your agenda and the board's agenda are at loggerheads. For example, the board may feel that your competence is in product development and therefore you should step down as CEO, concentrate on product development and innovation. They may insist on hiring a new CEO of their choice. This kind of disconnect has the potential of being a firecracker and destroying everything that has painstakingly been built in the organization. Again, having a mentor helps you ride this one out smoothly.

Pick someone who can give you time

You may have a member who has huge corporate brand equity, but by virtue of that he travels 300 days a year and you are not able to reach out to him for any counsel. What is the point of having someone like that? Yes, it does have much brag value, but do you want just this from him and not expect any insights or inputs? You may have one such member but you need to have members who can give you the time of the day. There are issues that can wait. There are issues that can't and you should be able to reach out to them in times of emergency.

How can the advisory board help you?

Credibility

As a young entrepreneur, let's accept it, you start out as a nobody. You are still a work-in-progress. You have a game-changing idea that is yet to be fully teased out in the marketplace. And, given the high mortality of startups, why should anybody take you seriously? This is where your board can lend you substance and standing.

Knowledge

It goes without saying that you have put together a cross-domain board for their competence. Together, that collective knowledge can spell sigma growth for your company.

I can share my own wonderful experience here. In 2011, when we started CARMa, the idea was to offer two products. One was mentoring which was my piece and the second was sachetized capital, which was the expertise of my co-founder. He had worked for a company in Australia, which offered a listing platform for companies in the early stages or those that were not yet qualified or ready for the listing on the stock market.

This platform, built on the Internet, acted like a mini stock exchange for such companies and the benefit was that it mobilized resources from small investors who had the opportunity of making money on the growth story. Simultaneously, it helped entrepreneurs access capital from an altogether new asset class.

We were very excited at what this product could do to the Indian entrepreneurial ecosystem. It never occurred to us that there could be any obstacles at all – certainly not of the legal kind so obsessed were we about doing good.

In our first board meeting, we proudly presented our product. We were expecting applause but instead, our Independent Director, Mr. Bharat Mittal told us that there was no legal framework, as yet, in India for a product like this and SEBI would never allow for it to happen.

All things considered, it was good that we had someone of Mr. Mittal's standing and knowledge on our board. It helped us pivot without losing too much money, time and effort.

Strategy

It has its roots in knowledge but it is more than just 'knowing' something; it has more to do with 'applying' what you know to a given situation and obtain the best possible outcome. Let me give you an example.

We have been mentoring 2800 illiterate women in Afghanistan for the last eight years, during which they have successfully built the largest *burkha* business in the world. It was a conscious decision, right at the beginning, to offer only high-end luxury products so it was natural that Saudi Arabia became our biggest customer.

About four years ago, I was invited as a keynote speaker at the Global Economic Forum conference held in Riyadh and accidentally, I was privy to a conversation which centered on Saudi Arabia wanting to become a WTO member.

The people who were having this conversation were women and they were hugely upbeat about what this would mean to them as one of the pre-requisites of this membership would be that the burkha should go.

Whilst I was rejoicing as a woman, I was also feeling devastated as a mentor! Because I knew that if Saudi Arabia was admitted as a WTO member, our biggest market for burkhas would die.

So I rushed back to Afghanistan, sat the women down and explained to them that we needed to come up with a new business idea quickly before we took a hit on the burkha business. Eight years ago, I had been the one to suggest that we should get into the burkha business. This time, the idea came from them. Why not make hummus and falafel and export it globally?

The point I'm making here is that knowledge, when applied to a given situation, yielded the strategy not just for survival but also a new opportunity.

Network

No amount of writing and discussion can emphasize the importance of the network that the board members can bring to the table. If you have 5 members on the board from different but complementary walks of life, each one can give you access to at least 10 men and women of solid brand equity (the kind who are on the jury of ET awards), at least a 100 well-known young guns, and at least a 1000 people who have either worked with them or been part of the same club or shared a hobby with. Not to mention the 5000 plus people who are connected with each of them on LinkedIn. And of course, at least, a 10000 of them who know of them. If this is the network each member can bring to the table, do your math as to what kind of network a board of 5 members can!

Just for this, I would be more than willing to pay a small fortune to my board!

How do you reach out to possible members?

If you are a student entrepreneur, the best way to access is through your college campus- take an active role in organizing events in your college to connect with the industry's stalwarts. It could be a management fest, an entrepreneurship conclave or a national conference. .

Then cultivate them in an unobtrusive manner (not by inundating their mailbox with unwarranted mails) by presenting an idea for their opinion, inviting them as jury for business plan competition or roping them as industry mentors for placements.

If you became an entrepreneur after tucking in some work experience, use your network and those of the others in your network, unabashedly to choose and approach.

In either case, what you are selling them is the possibility, the potential. Tell them in no uncertain terms that you need them on board to make it a reality.

How many members should you have on your Board?

There is no formulaic number but a board of six members should be a good one. The maximum should be 10. It is quite likely that when you raise money from VCs, they will expect a seat or two on your board. So besides them and the co-founders, it is good to have five to six people. It is not that you have to get them all in at the same time. You can bring them on board as and when you find the right fit. But keep looking from day one!

How do you remunerate the board members?

You have the option of offering them a retainer fee or giving them equity in your company. If the board members are meeting once a quarter, you also have to take care of their travel, transport and accommodation. Some companies also pay a small fee of Rs 10,000 per visit for the time spent in the board meeting in addition to flight and accommodation expenses.

If you are offering equity, it could range anywhere between 2 to 4 %, I have not come across an instance of equity being more than 5%. But it is hard to obtain information on this as these things are neither discussed nor documented openly. What I am discussing here is my own personal experience as a mentor.

How often should the Board meet?

Once a quarter is the ideal frequency for the board to meet– whether physically or virtually. It is always good if the entrepreneur can calendarize the meetings for all four quarters at the beginning of the financial year. It helps the members plan their travel and appointments beforehand.

Every meeting should have an agenda template for the quarter and it should be circulated among the members at least three weeks in advance. It is also very important that all documents regarding the agenda too are shared with the members at least a week before so that all the members come prepared.

A typical agenda may include the following:

- ❖ Minutes of the previous meeting
- ❖ Performance during the last quarter – budget vs. actuals
- ❖ Projected performance for the current quarter
- ❖ Product development pipeline
- ❖ New product launches
- ❖ Customer acquisition
- ❖ Customer attrition
- ❖ New hires, employee attrition, current status
- ❖ Capital deployment, return on investment, financial discipline
- ❖ Statutory compliance
- ❖ Events and news
- ❖ Branding and brand collaterals
- ❖ Any other

Whilst these items are a must, from time to time, you may choose to add other items which you may want to table for discussion.

Every board meeting should be minuted, preferably by a senior member of the team. The ideal person to do the minutes is the company secretary but if you don't have one, the next best person is your head of finance.

The minutes have to be circulated and approved by all the members before they are admitted as final. It is good to have the same person doing the minutes every time because it affords continuity, safe storage and retrieval.

The template for the minutes should also be standardized. For the last 20 years, I have used the one handed down to me by my English boss. It is simple, effective and efficacious. Each company can develop one that suits its unique purpose.

Summary

Like I said right at the beginning, the advisory board is the intellectual capital that will power your growth. Use it wisely and strategically. Don't expect your board members to get involved in operations but if you are having trouble, let's say with a truant employee, it may not be a bad idea to get him or her to meet with one of the board members.

Once, many years ago, one of my A-list customers was threatening to terminate our contract because we asked for a mid-term price increase (that would have been disastrous for us as he was a prominent expatriate who was hugely influential in his country's business group and almost 25% of our revenue came from that group). I requested one of our Board members, who was of the same nationality, to intervene.

We didn't get the percentage increase we had asked for but we got increase and most importantly, he did not terminate the contract. I was young at the time and when our board member told me that the customer was willing to give only a 5% price increase, and not 10% like we had asked for, I had felt let down and told him that it was unacceptable. Fortunately for me, the board member was a man who had seen the world and plenty of people like me in his lifetime. He gently told me that in a negotiation, you should give some and get some!

Sometimes when I look back on my own career, I can't but be thankful that I was fortunate in having wonderful teachers (starting with my father) who introduced me to the magical world of books; amazing bosses who groomed me; wise people who mentored me and peers, students, and mentees who taught me. I would always tell my father that God must have been in a very good mood when he made me!

TAKEAWAYS

- Like in most things in life, there is a right time to put together an advisory board. Take your mentor's help to identify that moment

- Put together a cross-domain team which has bought into your idea

- Remember that the board is in your corner. But if at any point they feel that you are the deal breaker, they will not hesitate to choose the company over you. And that is the way it should be

- If for whatever reason you don't get along with one of the members of the board, handle the matter judiciously and gracefully. Don't take to twitter to announce how glad you are that he resigned!

- Look at the advisory board as your third eye. For it to function effectively, make sure you are completely transparent in keeping the members in the loop on all matters.

SUTRA XVIII

THE ART OF
NEGOTIATION

66 I'm not going to negotiate with you – said
the Master of the dog (*he has the leash in his hand*).
Then I'm going to pee on the carpet, said the dog 99

– A cartoon

THE DICTIONARY DEFINITION of negotiation is 'mutual discussion and arrangement of the terms of a transaction or agreement'. This definition somehow makes it seem that we negotiate only in business. The truth is that we negotiate every minute that we are alive and breathing (and in today's smog-ridden world, we are even furiously negotiating with death every time we inhale).

As an entrepreneur, your journey is a long and convoluted series of negotiations. The travesty is that negotiation pre-supposes that both parties are interested in a dialogue. But, you will soon realize that everyone out there seems to think that as an entrepreneur who is just about to build your business, you are fair game for every kind of threat, blackmail, and submission. That's what makes your journey one of excitement and brinkmanship. The more you come to the negotiation table, the faster you will mature as an entrepreneur and leader.

With yourself in the mirror

Your first negotiation begins even before you join the race. Should I give in to this madness of building my own business? Should I play it safe and join a MNC which has made me an offer? Big salary, international brand, peer credibility and family pride– it will all come with the MNC packet. Conversely, none of that will happen with my entrepreneurial foray. Why am I even considering this when it is not a level playing field? What if I fail?

With your family

Let's assume that you won the negotiation with yourself. The next is coming up with winning arguments with your parents, spouse and other family members as to why you think this is a good decision. This one is really hard because it is the worst kind of emotional blackmail and in all probability, you have women at the other end of the deal table. They will use every tool from their arsenal – both heart and head.

One of the suggestions I have had – and it has worked every time – is to buy time. Let's say your mother is yelling at you for sitting out of placements, how could she possibly deal with the smug look of Anu Aunty whose son has just been recruited by an MNC and they have promised to send him to the US for two years? Especially when everyone knows that Anu Aunty's son is an idiot and her son was always so intelligent?

Listen to her tirade and then say:

Ok mom, I hear you. You are absolutely right; I'm much brighter than him. That is why I have this brilliant idea and not him. So let's do it this way. Give me one year's time to tinker with my idea. If nothing meaningful comes out of my tinkering, I will take up a job. This one year will be treated as my experience in starting a company so it will be considered a precious experience on my resume. So if it doesn't work, I can always go back to a job, but this time when I go back, it won't be as a fresher but as a failed entrepreneur who has garnered great experience of building a business around his idea. So I will join the company at a higher level and a better salary Who knows I might even join as Anu Aunty's son's boss!

It works and how!

With your co-founders

In early days, the parleys were almost enjoyable. Sitting in the college canteen, playing around with a number of different ideas, finally choosing that one shark of an idea and deciding to go ahead with it – there is a magic, a romance to this that has to be experienced.. It might fizzle out (more often than not, it does, as sanity prevails) but one odd time, the idea grabs your imagination in a vice-like grip and you start taking it seriously. So you sit out of placements and you negotiate with yourself; you buy time from your parents and now is the moment of reckoning.

You were part of a group that came up with this idea and started to flush it out. How many are as serious as you to take an idea forward and build a successful business around it? Typically, chances are three will drop out in a group of five and their excuses may range from, my folks will have a heart attack to I have to pay back my student loan. I'm being harsh in saying these are excuses, as, in all likelihood, they may be genuine reasons.

Only one other, besides you, is willing to be your cohort. He may stay either because he thinks it is a lark or he may stay because he is as passionate about the idea as you are. If it is the former, you will lose him at the first hint of trouble and that could be in the proto development stage itself.

If you don't lose him, now is the time to negotiate other important things. Like, how much equity stake in the company is he expecting? How much capital will he be able to bring to the table? What role does he see for himself? What happens if things don't pan out as expected? Will we be as great business partners as we are friends? Do we have to stop being friends, if we become business partners?

This negotiation is at the ideation stage. Once you do become co-founders, and go to market, the negotiation can center around just about everything to do with business; the products you build, the talent you hire, the organization culture you foster, the capital you raise, the revenue you generate, the profits you make, and even the exit terms, in case one of you decides to call it a day.

Let me illustrate this with an example. One of my mentees (let's call him A) approached me to negotiate his cofounder's exit. The two ran a highly successful advertising agency. They had been kindergarten friends, grew up in the same neighborhood, joined the same college and started business together. They ran it successfully for five years until B (his co-founder) decided to move on.

A was under the impression that the exit would be smooth and everything would be wrapped up in a jiffy without much hullabaloo. Until B walked in with a hotshot contract lawyer from one of the big firms, to our first meeting .

Thereafter everything spun out of control. The valuation, which was offered by B's lawyer made no sense, yet A wanted to accept it and pay a fortune to buy out B. So I had very little to do but play ball.

On the given day, when both parties were to sign the agreement, I was boiling. I knew A was being taken for a nice ride and I was frustrated. I was more vexed by the fact that A seemed pretty nonchalant about it.

We had all the documents ready for the buyout. And then, I don't know what got into me (my sense of fair play I guess). I pulled out the valuation documents from my bag, put them on the table in front of B's lawyer, looked at B pointedly and asked him to sign the documents. Without as much as looking at the paper, B signed. His lawyer looked on, smug as ever.

I smiled at B and his lawyer and said: *now you buy us out!*

This is called shotgun negotiation where you turn the table on someone. Of course I was called a number of names by the lawyer and B but the long and short of this negotiation was A, at the ripe old age of 33, was in a position where he now had so much money that he could comfortably retire to the Bahamas.

With your partners

It is a given in today's world that you need not build your business alone. You don't have to reinvent the wheel. For example, if you are an online travel portal, your only focus should be on bringing the buyer (customer interested in traveling) and seller (all the providers of services such as ticketing, accommodation, local transport, entertainment, activity and payment gateway) together on your platform. What they do and how they do what they do is all plug and play or as it is famously known in the Internet language API (Application Program Interface) integration.

Not just this, even to create your platform, you have partnered with providers of your cloud server, domain, web development, app development, ERP, CRM, business tools, recruitment portal, even partners for co-branding[1], may be even with crowdfunding platforms.

---

[1] for example, you may be one of the sponsors for a marathon that promotes 'have money, will travel' philosophy

Imagine how much time and resources would be consumed if you had to develop every piece of this yourself. So make the full use of it. Some of your partners may be mature entrepreneurs who may also bring their network to you. That network may be invaluable to you and will give a head start to your business in terms of your early paying customers, synergistic service providers or even for opportunities that you never thought of. And if they are recognizable brands, they in turn will lend enormous credibility to your business.

For example, one of my mentees who runs a chain of dental clinics has partnered with premium spas and five-star hotels to offer teeth whitening procedure to foreign tourists at their sites. When he set up his clinic, this was nowhere on his radar. He's now looking to set up a similar facility at airport lounges. I'm sure his company, Studio 32, will very soon become a pan-India brand.

So your negotiation tactic has to be different with different people. If you are negotiating with another young incumbent like you, barter away instead of hard cash changing hands. If it is a mature partner, then factor in how else you can leverage the partnership.

I always say this: as a non-negotiable rule, partner with strength. Your immediate cost may be high but your opportunity loss and the financial impact of that over the next few years can be easily contained.

With employees

I saw a lovely cartoon on negotiations that showed a snake refusing to dance to the snake charmer's *'pungi'* (a reed instrument made from gourd). As the hapless guy looked on, the snake said: I would like to renegotiate our terms!

To my mind, this is the trickiest of all and if you learn to negotiate with your employees and come out shining, you truly are a great leader.

The reason this is the trickiest is that there is much too much hype about employee engagement and motivation and way too little by way of establishing base lines and ground rules. As a result, the employees feel unreasonably entitled and the organization feels obsessively process driven and never the twain shall meet.

The negotiation starts with your first hire. Should I hire someone I can afford even if he isn't the brightest bulb in town? Should I hire the best possible talent by engaging him in a conversation of possibility? How can I get him to convert it into a conversation for action? At what point in time should I offer him equity? Is it during the interview so that it compensates for the poor pay? Is it when I'm suitably impressed with him and reward him with some equity in the company?

Do I want him to stay with my company forever or am I happy bringing people of different caliber at different points in time to get the best out of them??

Do I want to foster a regimented organization culture where behavior is governed by standard operating procedures (SOP) or should it be a completely freewheeling, fashionably anarchic culture which gives primacy to creative freedom? And if creative freedom is given primacy, how much freedom is too much?

This is a labyrinthine process of negotiation; at best exciting and at worst, shattering. I can tell you this. There are no easy answers to any of the questions but tripping on any of these can write the epitaph for your organization.

With your customers

It is interesting that the two of the three most critical pieces of your entrepreneurial journey (the third being your product) are actually hazardous to your health and the health of the organization you wish to build!

Let's say, you have built an enterprise product. And your potential customers are large-sized companies. Your negotiation starts from trying to get an appointment directly with the decision maker, the CEO of the company, and not someone down the line.

It goes on from one negotiation table to another, thereon. Here are some samples.

I want to pilot the product with your company; will you please give us money upfront so that we can use that money to develop a better product for you?

The price that you are willing to pay does not even cover my costs, could you please increase it?

How can I sign a service level agreement (SLA) with you that says I will give you all our product enhancements absolutely free for three years? (You end up signing anyway)

According to our terms, you were supposed to pay us in advance, it is six months since the product has been deployed at your offices and we still haven't received payment. (They will pay you only when they run out of excuses, if at all)

What do you mean you won't pay because our product is not working when everyone in your office is using it? (That's the conspiracy between the purchase and accounts department, delay tactics)

And how can you deduct 25% from our invoice on account of a month's delay in deploying the product? There is no such clause in the SLA. (It doesn't matter that there is no such clause, more delay tactics)

All books on entrepreneurship wax eloquent on how and why entrepreneurs should hook customers to their products. No one talks about why big dogs bite! The large customers should actually play a nurturing role towards startups to give them a head start as it were. Maybe they should have new diversity laws which say that startup entrepreneurs should be given preferential treatment, not singled out for harassment!

With Investors

This is the most one-sided negotiation ever. The entrepreneur is desperate for money and so even the most unreasonable terms are negotiated without a qualm. Low valuation against high equity stake is not the only double whammy. I have seen an investor agreement that said that if the co-founders do not perform as per the business plan, they might be fired with a month's notice! And the co-founders, six of them, actually signed it without even knowing that there was such a clause. They came to know about the clause when they were fired!

It is very important that the co-founders should have a contract lawyer on their side when they negotiate the agreement with investors.

With your Board

This negotiation starts only after your Series A funding. As an entrepreneur, how do you retain your freedom to bring competent people to your advisory board (the investor has a huge say here), who will also be in your corner if push comes to shove? Do you pay the members some kind of retainership or would they be happy to sit in on the board as it affords them ringside view of an exciting growth story? Typically, what should be the composition of the Board? What and how can you leverage their knowledge and network to catapult your organization into the big league?

The Why of the negotiation with your stakeholders

Basically as an entrepreneur, be ready for a series of negotiations with everyone in your ecosystem. Negotiation is also a strategy and like all strategies it has to be aligned with your larger purpose. In this sense it is long term.

Negotiation is also in here and now; in that it is just as much a short-term strategy. And if you don't get this one out of the way successfully, there may be no long-term at all.

For instance, if your first customer is a large marquee brand, you may negotiate a price, which just covers your basic cost. Your team may chide you for being overenthusiastic to onboard this customer.

Your reason for doing this may be two-fold – the obvious one that having a big brand as your first customer gives you brag value and makes it easy for you to acquire more customers.

But the second reason which is as practical as it is brilliant, is that for the next one year, during the contract term, you don't have to worry about paying your bills and that leaves you to focus on other critical things such as product enhancement, acquiring other customers at better prices and putting processes and systems in place.

So when you negotiate, it is not a knee-jerk reaction to a situation but behavior that is well thought through and holistically. You can't negotiate to win today and hope that tomorrow pans out. You are in the business for the long haul (I can't resist borrowing a phrase from Amitabh Bachhan's dialogue here *lambi race ka ghoda*, that is, a horse that is in it for the Derby) and every action you take or don't take has an implication either in the long term or the short term.

Your test of mettle as an entrepreneur is how well you balance it out, without sacrificing one for the other.

After 20 years in corporate and 10 years as a teacher and a mentor, I have found that some simple truths work in most negotiations. Let me enumerate them for you:

Do your homework

Before you get to the negotiation table, make sure you know everything there is to know about the other party. You should have such a detailed profile of the guy that even his own mother will find it difficult to recognize him!

This comes in handy, especially if you need to use leverage at a point when negotiation has hit what is called the Mexican standoff, that is, a situation where both parties are unwilling to budge.

It is also useful to establish what the other party hopes to gain from the deal. In my experience, there are always tangible deals which are evident and intangible ones which are subsumed. Extract the intangible ones to address them.

Many years ago, we had a situation in one of the companies that I worked for that best explains this. We had just commenced our operations in about five countries in the Middle East. We identified one of our senior guys as the ideal head for the operations.

This gentleman used to report to the vice president of international operations, who in turn reported to me. One day, the vice president came to my office looking puzzled and angry. He told me that he had spoken to O (let's call him O because A or X is too clichéd) about the promotion and he expected the guy to be positively delirious with happiness, but instead he had turned it down. The VP was apoplectic, to say the least.

I called O and spent half-an-hour with him trying to understand his reasons for turning down such a lucrative career opportunity. I knew he was single and that made his decision even harder to understand.

O's body language told me three things. One, he was petrified. Two, he was angry that we were moving him out of a role in which his performance was exemplary. Three, he was defiant. He was very sure that nothing would induce him to take up the offer.

I did not persuade him further as I wanted time to understand what was making him so frightened as it seemed that fear was the real driver of the rest of his behavior.

After much mulling, I arrived at a possible answer. It was a huge risk going back to him with my suspicion because if I was wrong, then we would have been in danger of losing him.

I took him out for a drink. We stayed off all work-related conversations during the whole evening. I talked of personal things – my daughter, a book that had captured my imagination and a joke that had made me laugh the hardest.

It was a delightful evening. He was very well-read, well-traveled, a wonderful conversationalist and had a quirky sense of humor.

He walked me back to my car and as I was about to get in. I took the chance of telling him, you can keep coming back to India every month you know. He looked puzzled at first and then shocked. I patted him on his back and got into the car.

O was gay and this story happened more than 18 years ago at a time when no one had come out of the closet. He was petrified that we would get to know of it, and he was even more petrified that in the Middle East which was known to be homophobic, he would not be able to survive. His biggest fear however was that it might be the end of the road for him and his partner if he agreed to move because he felt not being able to meet each other often would put huge pressure on their relationship.

O came back to me a week later telling me that he was ready to move to the Middle East. I'm guessing he made arrangements for all the pieces to fall in place.

What had I done here to make it a successful negotiation? Firstly, I had addressed upfront the one big fear he had – that we in the organization would get to know about it. By telling him that I knew, I was also telling him that it was a secret to which only I was privy and it would remain that way. That gave him the courage to address other issues.

Secondly, in telling him that he could come back to India every month, I was actually assuring him that he would get to meet his partner regularly. Both put together drove his demons away and he took the decision that proved to be the turning point of a very successful career.

Show empathy

I know it is very tempting to decimate the other guy at the deal table and if you have some advantage in the negotiation, you could do that too. But avoid it. A good negotiation is one where both parties go home thinking they won. This is not a fairy tale. It actually happens. Empathy is the biggest driver here. Let me share a story here.

Many years ago, in one of the companies I worked in, I had to fire a senior manager for non-performance. It caused some bad blood as he was well liked by his team. He was a typical 'come on boys lets go for a beer' kind of guy. So when we fired him, a number of people came to me with their resignation. It was important that we do damage control. In fact, even when before I fired him I knew that it would cause some unrest, as I was aware that he was high on popularity charts. What I hadn't expected however was that many of our key customers would rally around for him!

So we had a situation. I had to address the concerns of both employees and customers. I spent time with each of them, clearly and crisply told them why we had to fire him. I was very careful not to trash him in any of these conversations. I simply said that whilst he was a very good guy, he did not have the zing, that extra edge, to grow the business and if the business doesn't grow, where would we all be, I asked.

I was open in all my communication with both employees and customers and after a month- long conversation, matters died down. But I was quite sure it still rankled amongst most of them.

The opportunity to salvage came in a rather unexpected and tragic way. About six months later, the gentleman died in an accident. I went for the funeral, met his wife, gave her a decent check to meet emergency expenses and offered her a job. She turned down the job but she said she wanted to start a business of her own, making leather wallets, so could we give her rent-free place for a while in our office? We supported her for two years and now I'm told she runs a very successful leather export business.

The biggest upside of this for our organization was that all the simmering unrest vanished overnight and the team came together to build our most profitable branch! Reason? They liked working for a company where the leaders showed empathy.

Having said this, not all negotiations have happy endings. But the intent that both parties must go home happy should be there.

Be prepared for the unexpected

To quote Sidney Sheldon, even the best-laid plans can come a cropper if you haven't factored how to bat a googly for a six! Let me give you an example.

Many years ago, my partner Bruce and I went to Botswana to negotiate with a gunrunner to lay down arms. We had a Swahili translator but it was a very frustrating experience because the gunrunner never spoke a word. Throughout the negotiation, he just had a daft smile on his face.

After 72 hours of painful, one-sided, conversation, the gunrunner suddenly came alive. He rattled off something and the translator looked increasingly uncomfortable. Finally he told Bruce: he says he is willing to lay down arms, but he has a condition. He wants you to leave the lady behind because he wants to marry her when he comes out of prison (the lady in question was me, of course)! It took us another 72 hours of negotiation to get him to understand that this lady could not be left behind because she was already married and even had a *mtoto* (baby)!

Have the women negotiate

I mean this seriously, as we are natural at this game, having negotiated all our lives to simply survive!

Continuing with the above example, after the first 72 hours, both Bruce and I felt something shifted in the air. Bruce thought the gunrunner was thawing. I felt that indeed something in the equation had changed but it wasn't the way we were expecting it. And true enough, the gunrunner had thrown this googly at us.

Bruce read the situation in the light of the outcome he wanted. Which was to get the gunrunner lay down arms who would then be packed off to prison and we could go home. I read the situation as: it can't be so simple, even if he agrees to lay down arms, will he extract a price for it?

Bruce thought like a man and I thought like a woman; I do believe our brains are wired differently. Truly, men are from Mars and women are from Venus.

Your attitude can't be: my way or the highway

This is especially so when one of the parties has a distinct upper hand. So he comes to the table, all set to call the shots.

And that is evident in his body language. He is a power dresser, brand conscious, thrusts his chest out, is extremely articulate and uses words to effectively decimate the other person (if his body language hasn't already intimidated enough). He uses animated gestures like jabbing, pointing, thrusting and banging the table. And he makes no bones about who is in charge here.

This is not called negotiation. It is called annihilation!

Keep a tab on the time

The fundamental principle of any negotiation is that it should be contained in time. In crisis-management situations, the thumb rule is to negotiate and put the issue to bed under 36 hours. The longer you take the more fluid the power equation becomes and you will lose whatever advantage you may have had in the beginning. Let me give you an example.

Let's say you are in an accident and you are the perpetrator of the accident. Your car banged into the car ahead of you at the traffic signal. You get out of the car and ask if the passengers in that car are fine. Then you say, I'm sorry, my foot slipped off the brake, thankfully the damage is not much, I suspect it will cost you about this much to get it fixed, here's the amount. Both of you go on your way without much ado or holding up of traffic.

Contrast this with a scenario where as soon as you banged into the car ahead of you, you get out of the car, yelling at him (*Why did you brake so suddenly you jerk!*).The other guy in turn yells at you that he braked because the traffic signal turned red and it is not his problem that you don't know that there is something called a brake in your car that has to be applied exactly under such circumstances!

When you start off in this fashion, there is only way it can go and that leads to the police station. And the moment other parties, like the police, are drawn into it you have already lost your negotiation mojo.

So move in on the deal with a little give and take! Don't prolong the negotiation under some misguided perception that the more you drag the sweeter the deal will be. Rarely do you win in such protracted negotiations and the opportunity cost may be humungous.

Give something unexpected

This one is always a winner. We all love surprises and at the negotiation table if you offer something completely unexpected, your generosity fetches you brownie points and it creates a huge amount of goodwill. Let me illustrate this with another story.

Many years ago, my boss dispatched me to Muscat with a stern order: don't come back without buying that company. *That* company was a firm that we had been trying to buy for more than a year and had been utterly unsuccessful. The baffling thing was that this company was up for sale and we saw tremendous synergy between their products and our business.

The Sheikh who owned the company saw it too. We were pretty much on the same page even on deal value. Yet, for more than a year, nothing had come out of these parleys, largely because the Sheikh was a wily, shrewd and sadistic businessman who seemed more interested in brinkmanship than closing the deal.

Several teams that had gone to Muscat to complete the paperwork reported that the dialogue would go word-perfect until the last day and the Sheikh would lull you into thinking that the deal was in the bag. Just before signing on the dotted line, he would spring a surprise – a clause here, a new word there – that would derail further discussions.

So my boss' order of 'don't come back without buying that company' was born out of hair-tearing frustration, consternation at the delay and the consequent loss of opportunity. There was also huge self-doubt on whether this was all one big wild goose chase with the Sheikh leading us up the garden path, all the while laughing his head off. My boss was one of those who liked to look 'good'; he liked to come out of any negotiation, smelling of roses. This deal, so far, stank of ineptitude on our part.

So off I went. As soon as I walked out of the arrival lounge in Muscat, I was whisked off into a limo and half an hour later, I walked into the personal chambers of the Sheikh, a cavernous office with parquet flooring. He was seated at the far end of the room and his whole demeanor was of disinterest and disdain. I walked towards him, conscious of the clatter my stiletto made against the parquet floor and feeling cold at the expression on his face. Even before I said hello, he curtly said: no negotiations with women, go back.

I tried to reason it out with him but to no avail. Finally I told him that whilst I loved my job I did not love it enough to change my gender to suit his convenience and that I would be at the hotel, in case he changed his mind.

I called my boss and gave him the lowdown. My boss cussed and swore that he would tell the mean, chauvinistic guy where to get off!

By evening I was back in the Sheikh's office and over the next three days, we completed all the discussions and documentation. All the while, the Sheikh pretended like I did not exist. He would look at my chair and make conversation (reminded me of one of

Agatha Christie's less popular protagonists called Mr. Pyne. He wouldn't look at the other party and talk, but had the disconcerting habit of, as Agatha Christie so enchantingly paraphrased: 'And then he addressed the teapot'). I pretty much remained the teapot.

Over the next three days, I learnt a lot. His shrewdness kept me on my toes and I was determined not to give him any room to bail out on the last day. And the signing off went smoothly and we now owned the company.

I went to his chambers to wish him goodbye and to tell him how much I had learnt from him. He seemed impassive. When I was about to leave, he said: come to my home by 7, I will send my car.

That put me in a tizzy, because in the Middle East, there is no culture of inviting business partners, especially women, home. I called up my boss.

In his typical style, he said, go, but make sure you don't become his 101st wife!

I had a delightful evening. His house was a sprawling mansion, he was a genial and concerned host. He had invited the Industries Minister, a couple of senior bureaucrats, a person who was the right hand man of the sultan. It was eclectic and delightful company.

When I said goodbye to him, he said something strange. He said: for the first time, I met a woman who is my match!

Why did he say that? What did I do right to get that kind of a reaction from him? Here's my take:

- ❖ I had done enough homework on the Sheikh. I had my team put together a huge dossier, which I had read on the flight, on my way into Muscat. I knew just about everything that I needed to know about him professionally and personally

- ❖ Knowing him, I played to his strength. Even when he told me to go back, I had just said, I'm sure you will change your mind by evening, as you know it is the right thing to do. I hadn't been impolite or arrogant or worse, I hadn't tried to be a feminist!

❖ I respected his culture. I would never attempt to shake hands with him, I dressed appropriately and I made it a point to like and be liked by his team

But I think the turning point came on the last day. I had come to know from our local sources that a large MNC was setting up shop in Muscat and in about three months' time, there would be a huge order for a product in the Sheikh's company which till then had not been doing well.

Keeping this in mind I had increased my offer price. The Sheikh was not aware of this development and just before signing, I shared this little nugget with him. I told him that we had come to know from reliable sources that this order was coming to us (no one else made that product) and it was only fair that we shared some part of the fortune with him.

There was a huge risk in telling him this, as two things could have happened. One, he may have changed his mind yet again about selling his company. Two, he might have upped the asking price.

But I knew the Sheikh had risen from a very disadvantaged background and prided himself on his sense of honor and fair play. He admired it immensely in other people too.

This really was the turning point. And my guess is this is why he reacted the way he did.

This negotiation tactic of mine certainly had a financial implication in the short-term. But we gained tremendously in the long-term because in the next one year, he facilitated our foray into

Dubai, Kuwait and Sharjah markets by connecting us to the right local business partners.

Summary

Negotiation is a very positive reinforcement for both parties. Keep it that way. Don't let it disintegrate into a power display or an ego trip. Just remember this, a good negotiation generates plenty of endorphins (which are feel-good hormones) and both of you should be able to ride high on them. Negotiation is all about attitude. Go to the table wanting that both of you should win, not you alone.

TAKEAWAYS

- Negotiation is a powerful tool and the best entrepreneurs are those who refine it to an art
- Groom women in your organization to take on crisis-management roles so that they can be brought to the negotiation table. This is a winning strategy
- Attitude is everything in negotiation. Your attitude should be one of a nurturer, not a hangman
- Empathy gets you really far in any negotiation

SUTRA XIX

THE SCIENCE OF
NETWORKING

> ❝ **The currency of real networking is not greed but generosity** ❞
>
> – Keith Ferrazzi

WHAT IS NETWORKING? It's a very fashionable word in the corporate sector. When an executive says he's busy at a networking lunch, it somehow makes him sound important.

As in many things, this word too has been imported to the entrepreneur's lexicon. However, over time, it has assumed ginormous importance in the entrepreneur's scheme of things so much that events are organized with fancy names like meet-and-greet, hobnob, munch-and-mingle and hook-line-and-sinker.

Typically these events are for the express purpose of networking and are organized by an apex body like The Indus Entrepreneurs (TiE), SMB Connect or Startup Saturdays or such initiatives. In the metros there are so many such events that it is very hard to track their calendar.

In Tier II cities, the apex industry body like the CII or the local chamber of commerce has a wing dedicated for the young ones in their midst. They may be called Young Entrepreneurs or Young Indians.

One of the best-known international organizations for business networking is BNI. Their weekly meetings are not just to exchange pleasantries over breakfast but to actually share numbers in terms of how much (value in monetary terms) another member has helped them in business and how much, they in turn, have helped others.

There are also branded international bodies like Entrepreneurs' Organization, which is an elite peer-to-peer network, exclusively for entrepreneurs, with several local chapters and strict membership criteria.

With the 'Start Up Stand Up' initiative launched by the Government of India, to give impetus to startups, many more people have jumped on to the bandwagon.

So what is networking? What do you do when you say you are networking?

I am sure the word originated much before telecom and computers, but when I googled history of networking, all I got was history of computer networking! My surmise is that the caveman did not network nor did the hunter-gatherer or even the farmer. I think it is a post industrial revolution phenomenon and overseas trade contributed to it.

Soon after the industrial revolution in the 18th century, it was no longer about producing for oneself and for exchanging your produce with your neighbor's. You no longer worked with your kinsmen, the people you knew and trusted.

You started to produce for people whom you had never seen before, in far-away land. So this brought into your life, a slew of unknown people – brokers, seafarers, investors, customers – and in the early days, you trusted them all blindly, but over time, after you had some bad experiences, you learnt to form a network of people whom you trusted.

So when the word assumed importance in our lives, it was essentially based on trust built over time.

This is not how we view network today at all. Now, network is all about opening doors. It is all about establishing connections which come in handy for growing the business.

For the entrepreneur, network is the magical 'open sesame' which gives him access to talent, partners, vendors and customers!

The advent of the internet gave networking a huge boost. Man was always a social animal. The internet made it possible for him to even share his solitude on the numerous digital platforms. Network acquired myriad hues with social media technologies.

What are social media technologies?

The word technology refers to the fact that it is Internet based. It is social because it connects multitudes of people and facilitates their interaction (although some may argue that in fact social media has made people more isolated). It is media because it has published content.

So what are the things you can do on social media? How does that help in networking? You can:

* **Share** videos on YouTube and pictures on Flickr, Pinterest and Instagram
* **Connect** with people on Facebook, Twitter and Gmail
* **Collaborate** on Wikis, Google Hangout and Google Chrome. In fact I love Google Jam on Chrome, which allows up to three people to jam online, even chose your own instruments!
* **Create** your own content on blogs and Tumblr (the difference between a blog and Tumblr is that the latter is

a micro-blogging and social networking site wherein you can combine text and pictures)

❖ **React** to stimuli in your environment using Rotten Tomatoes (movie-rating site) and Burrrp (event/restaurant-rating site)

❖ **Categorize and organize** content using hashtags (just add the # to your content and it will tag all similar content in your network), Stumbleupon (create categories like music, jokes, fiction, etc.), and Delicious (which allows you to bookmark not just on your laptop but on web so all those who are browsing can see them)

❖ **Consume** content using a RSS (Really Simple Syndication where content comes to you, for example, ESPN Cricinfo sends cricket updates to your mobile), widgets (which sit on your device and gives you updates, for example, a weather widget) and torrent sites (from where you can download movies, clippings, music)

❖ **Mobilize** a crowd, applaud and create huge visibility (Thunderclap)

Broadly, all of the above can be labeled as social media technologies.

How is social media different from other media?

❖ It is viral, that is, it can reach a huge number of people in the shortest possible time

❖ It is engaging, that is, you can maintain high interest levels by using content strategically

❖ It is cost effective, that is, whilst it costs money it does not cost as much as print and TV and considering its potential for reach, it is the most bang-for-the-buck tool

In a business context, these properties of social media can be effectively exploited to:

* Acquire new customers
* Retain existing customers by engaging them; and
* Getting existing customers to acquire new customers (this is where you maximize your benefit. You don't go around spending money on acquiring every single customer. You spend on one and keep him seduced and he will bring the next customer and so it grows virally)

So today's mantra is network or perish!

Why do you network?

You network for all the business reasons mentioned below:

* To create awareness about your product
* To acquire customers, and
* To engage with your customers

You do this to gain mindshare of your customers so that they make you a marquee brand. You may also network for purposes of hiring talent for your organization.

You also network for your own personal branding (check out some of the profiles on LinkedIn, the multi-skill endorsement, the display makes you think that India is a land of corporate geniuses), for seeking career opportunities, for collaborating on a hobby or passion (bikers' groups, musicians' *baithak*, artists' *adda* and the like). You may also network to find a date, a companion or a spouse (Shaadi.com, Tinder, Trulymadly, Woo).

Whether it is for your organization or for yourself, you network for branding, engagement and visibility. So you network because you can and you must.

Networking, as a verb, has gained currency because it is woven around the three R's – reduce risk (you can run ideas by others and take their counsel), reuse insights (you can learn from their mistakes), and recycle experience (you can add your own learning to it to make it better).

In other words, you network to create awareness, to collaborate, to forge partnerships, to improve mindshare, to curate and to change the rules of the game.

How does networking work?

It is a magical web of directed communication. It is credible, far-reaching, purposeful and result-oriented. Over the last decade or so, it has almost been honed into a science. Hence I called this chapter, the science of networking!

Let's now look at some of its elements:

❖ **It is vital**. We have already established that. The world around us is changing at a frightening pace. The shelf life of most products and technologies is very limited. In the past, there was no major difference between the African hand axe made 285,000 years ago and one made 250,000 years later. Today, a technology or product which was top-of-the-mind, a decade ago, may have been consigned to history. For example, VCR's, cassette recorders, pagers, even palm pilot and dial-up Internet

So if we need to be on top of this fast-paced change, we need to be networked.

❖ **It is virtuous.** By and large, it is a good thing. It can become bad if not moderated or controlled. For example, the whole Maggi episode in India in 2015 spiraled out of control because Nestle, the owner of Maggi chose to maintain stoic silence. They probably thought, misguidedly though, that if they don't add to the conversation, the conversation would die down. May be this strategy would have worked with some products. But with Maggi, its customers have a huge emotional connect; hence the strategy of silence boomeranged

An interesting story regarding singer Susan Boyle is a good example of virtuosity. In 2012, her PR team ran a twitter campaign for her new album called Standing Ovation. The hashtag was #susanalbumparty!

It may have left Susan Boyle red–faced but it was one of the most retweeted posts of the year and the most trending topic worldwide, hugely boosting the sales of the album.

❖ **It is viral.** This is a given. The reason you network is for the 'wild fire' effect. Network typically has three layers. Your primary contacts are those where you know someone personally; your secondary contacts are those whom you don't know personally but they are connections of your primary contact; your tertiary contacts are those which are the connections of each of your secondary contacts. So the multiplier effect is huge, quick and purposeful

Let me give you an example. Let's say you want to develop a mobile app for your product. You contact a friend (primary) who works for a large technology MNC. He refers you to someone who is the brother of his colleague (secondary) who has quit CISCO and started a mobile app development company. You find him too expensive but he in turn suggests that he knows someone who is a good app developer and you could possible hire him (tertiary).

When you develop a relationship with the secondary and tertiary contacts, they move into your primary contact layer. This exercise is a self-perpetuating one and exploited very effectively by companies that use multi-level marketing (MLM) for their products, such as Amway, Tupperware, Modicare and others.

> ❖ **It is virtual.** Internet has made it possible to network effectively because you can now do it online. Physical networking would have imposed a number of restrictions in terms of time, effort and money. But online cuts across spatial and temporal barriers and makes networking easy, efficient and productive

Let's say you made a trip to Everest base camp. In the physical model, you could tell about it to a few people whom you came across, mostly face-to-face. Now you can post pictures on Facebook and Whatsapp; you can review your whole experience on Tripadvisor; you can hashtag #myeverestbasecamp and send out real-time tweet to people in your network. As long as you have data connectivity (in my experience, you have the best connectivity in these places, we had at 18,000 feet in Khardung-La in Leh, and at 21,000 feet in Dolma La in Kailash), you can capture every snowflake real-time on your trip!

So it is an interesting combination of things. One, it tells your network that you are on your way to Everest base camp. Two, and more important, it shows a side of you that is different from what your professional connections knew about you. This dimension of your personality makes them see you with new eyes, maybe they will even like you better.

I have experienced this personally. In my professional career,

I'm known for being a teacher and a mentor. The way I dress generally gives the impression of a flamboyant, young-at-heart woman. So the impression most people have of me is of a 'cool' professional. When they come home, the fact that I am obsessively house-proud takes them by surprise. And when they see me cook, the reaction is always the same: you cook like my mother but you don't look like my mother!

And thereafter I see a whole shift in our equation. They see me as a person and not just in my professional role. That becomes hugely rewarding for both of us.

As we have already seen, your mentor is a huge source of network and you should leverage it at all stages of your entrepreneurial journey.

The virtual aspect of networking is a phenomenal facilitator of both business and personal relationships. Social media platforms like LinkedIn have created a rewarding experience for its members.

Who should network?

The butcher, the baker and the candle stick maker! Literally everyone because as I said earlier, networking comes easy to humans as man is a social animal. The advent of Internet has made networking more structured, the access easier and more democratized.

What you should not do in the name of networking

Don't stalk!

Just because access is easy, it doesn't mean you bombard someone on social media platforms, through mails, messages and even calls.

Don't troll!

Let us say you did not have an interaction with someone the way you expected. Don't take to social media to start a hate campaign.

Don't insist on a visiting card!

There are a number of people who do not give out visiting cards. I don't because all my contacts are available on the Internet. So when I say I don't have cards, the typical response is can you write down your phone number and email id? This is irksome in today's world when most professionals have a solid digital footprint.

Don't spam!

Just because you now have access to my mail or social media, don't inundate with your mailers. Politely ask first if it is ok to send a company brochure or mailer. Only after that, do the needful. And after mailing the brochure, don't send ten mails in quick succession saying, "I have sent it, have you read it! Don't be a pest."

Don't share!

Don't give out details of people in your network without first checking up with them. If someone wants to be connected to someone else in your network, first ask, give the background and only after the person gives you the go ahead should you do a connecting mail.

Don't intrude into personal space!

If you have networked with someone on LinkedIn, don't send overly familiar personal emails. I have experienced this many times. I am asked whether I would like to meet up for coffee, go for a movie or even a holiday! I once even received a marriage proposal from a guy in Dubai. He wrote to me saying he had heard me speak at an event and decided that I was just the right companion for him. He was already married with a 4-year-old son, but he promised me that he would build a first floor for me in his house! And all of this on LinkedIn!

Summary

Networking is a powerful tool. Use it judiciously and efficaciously to grow your business. Like all tools, its effectiveness is in how you use it. Don't abuse it.

TAKEAWAYS

- Network is your business circuitry. It is a complex web of connections and prospects. It can open doors that would be firmly shut otherwise

- There are plenty of opportunities to network, from the physical (events) to the virtual (social media platforms). Each is governed by a set of rules. Respect them for your own good

- Social media offers a powerful platform to network in general. But you may want to pick and choose those platforms that are aligned to what you wish to achieve. So first identify your reason for networking in a given situation

- Don't spread hate, lies or animosity in your network. It will come to bite you in the ass

SUTRA XX

JUST DO IT

> **It does not matter whether you win or lose, until you lose**
>
> – John McEnroe

WE ARE LIVING IN the SMAC (Social, Mobile, Analytics, Cloud) era. Social has changed the way we connect with the world. Mobile has given us power in the palm of our hands. Analytics has made us the center of the universe. Cloud has taught us a new way to consume information.

Not just the Internet but Internet of Things (IoT) is also changing the way we live. Between SMAC and IoT, startups are challenging large, established organizations forcing many of them to either reinvent themselves or acquire startups to give them the necessary relevance in the marketplace.

Recently, Cisco made a strategic decision to buy Silicon Valley based Jasper Technologies for $1.4 billion. Jasper is in the business of IoT devices. Cisco is a behemoth in making equipment that connects machines and networks to the Internet. The acquisition will widen their product offering to include devices that helps people manage jet engines and vending machines on the Internet.

I know that there is plenty of buzz about entrepreneurship in India. Everyone is talking about unicorns. Don't get carried away by that. If you set out to build a unicorn, you will end up with a unicorpse (I read this somewhere on the Internet, was amused by it and couldn't resist using it here!). Building a unicorn cannot be the reason for your entrepreneurial journey. It has to be at best, an unintended consequence of doing large-scale good.

Entrepreneurs like you have made this possible. Entrepreneurs like you, who are selfish and set out to change the world, make it into a better place; all because you did not like the world you lived in. You chose to change it, because you could. In the process, you affected so many lives for the better. You wanted your tomorrow to be better than your yesterday. You made our tomorrows better than our yesterdays.

Technology today has democratized access and I think at no other point in human history has it been possible to do so much good in so little time. In the past, my local grocer knew that I bought Dabur honey only during the winter months because he knew I drank lemon and honey in warm water, first thing in the morning. He knew I avoided drinking this in summer. If he did not see me for 3 days on the trot, he would send his six-year-old son to check if everything was all right with me.

When the super markets came, we all lamented that we had lost that personal touch. No one knew who we were, no one cared what we bought, whether we bought.

Now technology has restored that intimacy with a bang. Amazon knows what books I buy and knowing that, Amazon recommends what I might like to read. I bought a pair of suede boots from Jabong and a month later, Jabong asked me if I wanted another pair but this time in leather. When I order Chinese take away from my neighborhood restaurant, the system flags that I am allergic to mushroom. And if I don't ask for a service from Urbanclap for a month at a stretch, I get a gentle nudge from them in my mailbox saying: we haven't seen you in a while!

So you have made our lives meaningful, convenient and self-contained, yet connected. I am sure the journey will not be the way you planned it. Even the best-laid plans go awry. But you have the staying power.

- ❖ Because you are driven by the need to make this world a better place
- ❖ Because you are inspired from within. I love the fact that the English word Entrepreneur and the Sanskrit word Antarprerna (inspiration from within) sound so similar!

That is exactly why you became an entrepreneur. To create meaning in society, to touch so many lives so that you became immortal.

Just do it. Like I said before, doing good looks good on you.

ABOUT THE AUTHOR

PROFESSOR NANDINI VAIDYANATHAN, Chairman and Managing Director, CARMa Venture Services.

She's a traveling teacher who teaches Entrepreneurship in several ivy league business schools around the world. From being just a word in the dictionary a few years ago, entrepreneurship has now consumed her whole being.

After 20 years in the corporate sector, working in MNC's on all inhabited continents, she returned to India in 2005 and began teaching entrepreneurship. But she realized that the only way she could bring real time experience to her classroom was if she became an entrepreneur herself. So she founded her company, CARMa (Creating Access to Resources & Markets), (www.carmaconnect.in) with a lofty ambition: to offer professional mentoring to entrepreneurs as a risk mitigating strategy. CARMa mentors start-ups, mature enterprises and family businesses. As on date, CARMa has mentored over 2000 entrepreneurs!

CARMa has also been involved in mentoring women to scale from livelihood enterprises to opportunity based and profitable

organizations in Afghanistan, South and East Africa and India. Till date over 10,000 women have been mentored to build scalable and profitable enterprises.

She is a prolific writer for mainstream newspapers, portals and blogs. She is a TED speaker and is regularly on the jury of television shows on business channels and entrepreneurship events across the world. She was named Business Woman of the Year by Business Goa in 2014.

Her book *Entrepedia*: A step by step guide to becoming an entrepreneur in India, is a huge best-seller since its launch in 2011. Its second edition, updated and contemporized, was published in mid 2015 and has become the bible of the start up community.

She loves cooking and entertaining people. She is also a trained Carnatic classical singer. She travels across the globe for teaching, mentoring, speaking, trekking and climbing. She currently resides in Goa.

* 9 7 8 8 1 8 4 9 5 9 1 8 5 *